A MILKWEED CHRONICLE

A MILKWEED CHRONICLE

The Formative Years of a Literary Nonprofit Press

Emilie Buchwald

MILKWEED EDITIONS

Published 2021 by Milkweed Editions
Printed in the United States
Cover design by Mary Austin Speaker
Cover photo/illustration by R.W. Scholes
Author photo by Dana Buchwald
Interior design by Bookmobile
The text of this book is set in ITC Galliard Pro
22 23 24 25 26   5 4 3 2 1
First Edition
ISBN 978-1-63955-047-0

Library of Congress Cataloging-in-Publication Data has been applied for.

Milkweed Editions is committed to ecological stewardship. We strive to align our book production practices with this principle, and to reduce the impact of our operations in the environment. We are a member of the Green Press Initiative, a nonprofit coalition of publishers, manufacturers, and authors working to protect the world's endangered forests and conserve natural resources. *A Milkweed Chronicle* was printed on acid-free 100% post-consumer waste paper by BookMobile.

This book is dedicated to writers and to readers
in the belief that literature is a transformative art, uniquely able
to convey the essential experiences of the human heart and spirit,
with the power to change the ways in which we respond to the world.

CONTENTS

– 1 –

A Milkweed Chronicle

– 49 –

The Milkweed Chronicle Prefaces

– 115 –

Milkweed Board Members, 1980–2003

– 117 –

Milkweed Staff, 1980–2003

– 121 –

Milkweed Editions Titles, 1984–2004

– 129 –

Acknowledgments

A MILKWEED CHRONICLE

"Milkweed seeds sailing on the winds, journeying . . ."

I WROTE THOSE WORDS in the winter of 1980 in an announcement for the first issue of the literary–visual arts journal *Milkweed Chronicle*. Happily, forty years later, milkweed seeds continue their flights into the lives of readers, and Milkweed Editions has developed a deep root system and a fine spread of leaves, vibrantly alive.

To celebrate forty years of literary publishing, I've written my part of the Milkweed story. I've distilled my thoughts about those intensely vibrant years, a grand adventure, into these relatively few pages. We launched the journal in 1980. Our first book came out in 1984. When I retired from the press in 2003, Milkweed had published 190 titles—recipients of more than two hundred prizes, awards, and recognitions—with more than a million books in circulation.

I continue to value every book I acquired, and therefore I regret that in this condensed account of almost a quarter of a century of publishing, I won't be able to mention nearly as many of our authors or titles as I'd wish to. I've described the start-up years of *Milkweed Chronicle* in detail, followed by discussions of the particular land-marks that contributed to the evolution of *Milkweed Chronicle* into the nationally recognized literary nonprofit publisher, Milkweed Editions. As an enrichment to the narrative, I've included the intro-ductory prefaces to *Milkweed Chronicle*, as well as the names of the board and staff members I had the pleasure of serving with.

In the 1970s and 1980s, major publishing houses in New York City were merging into publishing empires, focused more on the business of producing best sellers than on publishing literary books. Those mergers stimulated the counter-rise of a new generation of literary evangelists, independent journals and small presses, each with a particular mission and esthetic. Though *Milkweed Chronicle* came into existence as little more than an enticing idea tossed back and forth between its publishers-to-be, we were a mission-driven journal from our inception.

In 1978, Randy Scholes and I were board members of a fledgling literary arts nonprofit organization, the Loft, founded in 1975 by a group of writers, literally in the loft of Marly Rusoff's bookstore near the University of Minnesota. Before Randy and I met, I had admired his beautiful drawings and bookplates at a Loft display. At the time, Randy was the head of the Loft art committee; in fact, he *was* the art committee. He was esteemed as a book designer and illustrator and for his years of work as head illustrator for the award-winning *Minnesota Daily*. I was an editor, a poet, and a children's book writer. During the years I was completing a doctorate in English literature, I taught literature classes at the University of Minnesota and, after that, poetry writing at the Loft and writing for children through the University of Minnesota's Continuing Education for Women program. Now, for the first time in years, I was not fully occupied by a job, graduate school, or family obligations.

It was early one afternoon before a Loft reading by poets Etheridge Knight and Robert Bly at the University of Minnesota's Coffman auditorium that Randy and I first considered the ideas behind what would become *Milkweed Chronicle*. Because the Loft board members took on whatever tasks needed to be done, including cleaning the old house that served as our office and meeting center, it didn't seem unusual to us that Randy and I were deputized to carry a table needed for the reading from the Loft headquarters at the edge of university property across the campus to the auditorium. As we walked, balancing the table between us, Randy and I began a conversation about the work of the poets we were about to hear, moving on to a more general conversation about poetry and book arts. We discussed the fact that, surprising to us, there were no magazines or journals that gave equal space and weight to literature and the visual arts or that featured regular collaborations between these art forms. We commented that such a journal could cross-fertilize both genres. It was an intriguing conversation, and we agreed to continue it.

During the next six months, over the phone and over burgers, we talked. And we investigated, searching for an American journal that combined literature and visual arts in a collaborative fashion. We found none. When we researched the past, we were inspired by European artists Wassily Kandinsky and Franz Marc, who wrote about the relationships possible between artistic disciplines. In 1912, they published a collection of text and art, *Der Blaue Reiter Almanach*, named for a painting by Kandinsky. They discussed how to connect artistic disciplines, exploring parallels between painting and other art forms, seeking the "correspondences," or inner sympathies, that existed between the arts. The journal Randy and I had in mind would attempt to do much the same, seeking parallels and relationships between words and images in our place and time.

We considered the content and format for this new journal. We agreed that each issue should have an overarching theme, a subject that afforded contributors great flexibility and a multitude of possibilities. We would encourage new as well as seasoned writers to contribute. Each issue would announce the themes for future issues, giving writers and artists ample opportunity to prepare submissions.

The journal's format had to be nontraditional to provide enough space for the collaborations we envisioned. We wanted to offer readers the novel experience of reading several poems or an essay and of viewing one or more pieces of art on the same page. We also wanted to be able to present text and art on a double-page spread to give the reader-viewer the opportunity to consider both the individual works and the impact of the total composition.

We spent a great deal of time in libraries—there was as yet no Google to consult—paging through magazines and journals, considering not only subject matter but also optimal page size. The usual magazine page was far too small for the effects we wanted to create. We realized that we needed a space that was around the size of a newspaper page to allow us to create visually exciting single pages as well as potent double-page spreads. We decided on the same width as a page of the *New York Times*, with a length six inches shorter. When pages of this size were open, we would have a double-page spread twenty-three inches across, a canvas that would afford a variety of opportunities for visual presentation.

We adopted a name that appealed to us. *Milkweed Chronicle* honored the sturdy, wild plant that I passed on my daily runs, the essential diet of monarch butterflies, a plant that thrived on little and was barely noticed until its ripe pods exploded in fall. The milkweed seemed to us a fitting emblem for the arts themselves: hardy enough to flourish anywhere and everywhere, and, when fully ripe, seeding the world with energy.

After months of planning, we were ready to proceed, but we paused to consider what we were proposing to do. Could we create this journal and sustain it? Neither of us had business or financial experience. On the other hand, between us we had years of practical, hands-on experience in writing and editing, design, and illustration. To go forward, the path that seemed the most sensible and the most appropriate was to incorporate as a nonprofit, a 501(c)(3) organization, which would give us the imprimatur to actualize our ideas. After we received notification of our nonprofit status, we began seeking financial support to begin.

We bankrolled our initial expenses with the royalties from my first children's novel, but we needed significantly more to manufacture the first issue. We began our funding search by approaching the Jerome Foundation, because of its remarkable history of investing in start-up arts organizations. I met with Cynthia Gehrig, the foundation president, to explain our plans and to ask whether we could submit a grant proposal. Cynthia listened; she asked incisive questions, including the likelihood of our venture's success. A few weeks later when I returned for a second meeting, I handed Cynthia a report documenting, among other facts, that 80 percent of literary journals went out of business within a year. Our report also provided a detailed financial budget and a three-year plan. The Jerome Foundation decided to award us a grant for the first issue—if we promised that there would be a second issue, a challenge we accepted.

I wrote to one of my favorite poets, William Stafford, about our plans to make poetry central to the journal. Stafford, a pacificist, former poet laureate, and winner of the National Book Award in poetry, was also a noted teacher and mentor of poets. Stafford wrote back, saying that he would be happy to talk to me about the journal during a brief layover in Minneapolis on his cross-country flight home from Washington, DC, to Oregon. During that all-too-brief hour in the airport lounge, he listened, asked questions, and offered suggestions. When he left to catch his plane, he said that he would be happy to introduce the new journal to his colleagues and students, and he generously gave us permission to use two of his poems in the first issue. One of these, "The Dream of Now," already held a place of honor above my desk.

The Dream of Now

When you wake to the dream of now
from night and its other dream,
you carry day out of the dark
like a flame.

When spring comes north, and flowers
unfold from earth and its even sleep,
you lift summer on with your breath
lest it be lost ever so deep.

Your life you live by the light you find
and follow it on as well as you can,
carrying through darkness wherever you go
your one little fire that will start again.

Is it grandiose to admit that we wanted our journal to be a small spark in the great darkness of the world, believing that the arts inspire, bringing light, joy, insight, and healing? Poets and writers remind us to live in the moment, in the "now" that is our particular experience of life, offering the wisdom that each of us has a way through the darkness, our "one little fire that will start again."

The agenda we set forth in the first issue of *Milkweed Chronicle* was not modest. The banner headline across the editorial page read, in thirty-point bold type: *Where Do We Come From? What Are We? Where Are We Going?* These questions are written in paint (in French) by the artist Paul Gauguin across one of his last and most exciting Tahitian paintings. They are questions That address what all civilizations ponder. Our goal was that each issue of *Milkweed Chronicle* should speak, in some way, to each of them.

We sent information to writers and artists, asking for submissions of poetry and essays for the first issue with its theme, "Myths—Open Doors." A few weeks later, our post office mailbox was full. Over the next months, we winnowed the submissions, a rich cache of contributions.

We paired the typeset poems and essays with art and began the process of assemblage, creating combinations and correspondences on those large, inviting pages. We found the results inviting, hoping that we would not be the only ones captivated. In the preface to the first issue, we asked the reader to "judge us by the height of the attempted. There will be failures of technique and failures of illumination. Sometimes an aspiring failure sets off more significant reverberations than an easy success."

In those days before desktop publishing and design software, Randy spent days cutting out and pasting down type and art on boards, one for each page of the issue, each one created individually by hand. When the first issue was ready, we drove for an hour to a suburban printing company to observe the pages being photographed and made ready to print. We watched as copies of the first issue of *Milkweed Chronicle* roared out of a gigantic newspaper printing press. Each issue was folded in half and wrapped in cellophane. We mailed them from the post office to contributors and to our first few subscribers. It was hard to believe: *Milkweed Chronicle* was a reality.

The first issue was reviewed positively in the Arts sections of both Twin Cities newspapers. We received letters of support, a number of them from editors and publishers of small presses. Readers were intrigued, some by the ways in which we explored the theme, others by the unusual format and the juxtaposition of text and art. Not long after publication, we heard from the Dayton Hudson Foundation—today the Target Foundation—that they would support the publication of the second issue. We were able to report to the Jerome Foundation, well ahead of schedule, that our commitment to produce a second issue would be fulfilled.

For the first years, *Milkweed Chronicle* lived the hand-to-mouth existence of a new nonprofit, surviving on small grants and a modest amount of subscription revenue. We compensated for our lack of cash with sweat equity. But it was that slender stream of nonprofit funding that made it possible for the journal to survive and to gain momentum. As one issue followed another, we continued to attract admirers and supporters. We received more submissions for each issue.

Board participation was a key factor in our early survival and ultimate success, as it has been throughout the existence of Milkweed Editions. Our first board members were friends, invaluable and indefatigable. One of them volunteered to prepare our financial statements for the first couple of years. After that, board members met with the first president of the McKnight Foundation and helped to secure funding for a part-time financial position.

Our lively participation in the Twin Cities community was another element in our favor. During the *Chronicle*'s first year, a year when I was the Loft board chair, we set up joint readings at libraries and independent bookstores. Randy and I held office hours with local and visiting authors and artists. We chose a local company to typeset the journal and, later, our books. We continued to print the journal in the Twin Cities suburbs. For two years, we were publicity managers for the Great Midwestern Bookshow, the first large assembly of midwestern presses, held on the east bank of the University of Minnesota campus. Local organizations expressed confidence in our sustainability by placing ads in each issue.

From 1982 until the *Chronicle* stopped publishing, we hosted fundraising cabarets billed as "Crockweed Manacles," evenings of lighthearted, occasionally zany author presentations that always attracted a full house. Board members invited their friends to attend. Prizes at these events included author-hosted dinner parties and author-donated literary coaching, or a reading by an author at the home of a donor.

During the 1980s, the Twin Cities were home to thriving artistic disciplines that included not only books and literature but also music, theater, dance, public radio and television, and the visual arts. Both the Minneapolis and the St. Paul newspapers employed staff reviewers who promoted homegrown authors and publishers on their Sunday book pages. The Loft was a mecca for writers, offering classes and grants. Libraries held readings for both adult and children's book authors. Both cities had thriving independent bookstores, favorite hangouts for readers. I browsed, far too long and far too often, at the Hungry Mind, Micawber's, Odegard Books, and Savran's, to name a few favorites that are no longer around.

Twin Cities foundations and corporations donated liberally to the arts. In addition, the Metropolitan Regional Arts Council and the Minnesota State Arts Board were a source of grants and fellowships for individual artists and for nonprofit arts organizations throughout the state. This ongoing financial support for the arts created stability for a flourishing hive of high-quality arts organizations.

The opportunity to receive grant support drew small press publishers Allan Kornblum of Coffee House Press and Scott Walker of Graywolf Press to relocate to the Twin Cities in the early 1980s, joining Norton Stillman's Nodin Press (founded in 1968, the first Twin Cities indie publisher) and Bill Truesdale's New Rivers Press. When the nonprofit Minnesota Center for Book Arts opened in downtown Minneapolis in 1983, their offices immediately became a nexus for book culture. Randy and I took a letterpress printing class at MCBA, easy for us to do because we could walk the few blocks from our office.

That small office in lower downtown Minneapolis was housed in the building known as the Hennepin Center for the Arts. This Romanesque building with its turrets and towers, built in 1888 as a

Masonic temple, had recently been renovated as an inexpensive rental space for arts organizations. In addition to working on the next issue of the journal, we dealt with the daily realities of office life: activities like answering phone calls, typing lists, communicating with authors, setting up files, mimeographing flyers on that ancient artifact, the mimeograph machine, and then distributing them, as well as, yes, cleaning up after ourselves.

The first week in our new office, Marilyn Matthews, whom we knew as a Loft volunteer, showed up and asked if she could become our *Milkweed Chronicle* volunteer, a stunningly generous offer. That afternoon Randy, Marilyn, and I sat together in our small space folding and sorting flyers. Marilyn offered to take the finished bundles to the post office and mail them. It seemed like a miracle that someone intelligent, kind, cheerful, and interested in what we were doing would appear as often as we asked and help us accomplish whatever needed to be done. She was a guardian angel from that first day until I retired from Milkweed Editions.

The following year, thanks to our grant from the McKnight Foundation, we were able to hire a part-time financial associate, though we listed her on our masthead more imposingly as business director. We convinced Marilyn Heltzer, on a sabbatical leave from Minnesota Public Radio, to take the job after a luncheon during which she learned, to her mingled wonder and horror, that I was keeping the subscription rolls on a series of yellow legal pads. A year later, after putting our financial systems in order, she returned to MPR, and we hired new sterling part-time help: Marilyn's daughter, Debby, became our subscription manager. Writers Paulette Bates Alden, Mary Ellen Shaw, and Lisa McLean became, respectively, business manager, copy editor, and public relations manager.

It wasn't until 1986, when we moved upstairs into two large rooms on the fifth floor of the Hennepin Center for the Arts, one of them a round turret room perfect for meetings with authors, that we had the means and the space to add two full-time coworkers. Steve Chase, an aspiring publisher himself, became our business manager, and poet and teacher Deborah Keenan, the essence of energy and productivity, became our managing editor. For the first time, the journal had a staff. We were busy and thriving. We enjoyed the work and our camaraderie; once a week or so, we walked to one of the many nearby restaurants for lunch.

I would like to believe that the major reason the journal survived was that we reliably produced and delivered three issues of *Milkweed Chronicle* a year for seven years, each issue displaying the work of more than fifty new and seasoned writers and artists. I was thrilled that we were publishing writing that was diverse and accomplished, writing that looked for and often found light in dark subjects, writing that tackled each theme with imagination and vigor. As we intended, *Milkweed Chronicle* was the first publication credit for hundreds of our contributors. During those years, the journal published over a thousand poems, essays, and works of fiction, as well as a variety of illustrations and artwork.

As I mentioned, the organizing principle of each issue was a theme that offered imaginative opportunities for writers and artists to explore. Randy and I researched and discussed that theme before I wrote the preface to introduce each issue.

Milkweed Chronicle went through relatively few physical changes over the years. With the Fall 1983 issue, we modified its size and shape to produce a shorter, thicker, stapled issue with a more distinctive two-color cover. For the Fall 1984 issue and afterward, we added a handsome color cover printed on gloss stock. While the content of *Milkweed Chronicle* continued to evolve, what didn't change was our desire to publish exceptional writing and visual art. When I read the literary submissions, I looked for the qualities that appealed to me as a reader: a vigorous individual voice that riveted me to the page or that made me pause to reflect. In our spacious pages we were able to publish complete chapbooks as well as sizable excerpts from forthcoming and in-progress novels and nonfiction titles. Over time, we recognized that the journal offered a precious opportunity to publish essays and articles about subjects we found meaningful in the areas of ethics, social justice, and the environment. What we didn't recognize at the time was that *Milkweed* already had an agenda on its way to becoming a mission.

The writers in our audience wrote and phoned (there would be no email for another two decades), informing us about their new work. Eventually, writers asked whether we would consider publishing their book-length manuscripts. Randy and I talked about this possibility. Why shouldn't we, why couldn't we, add books to our publishing program? We had an audience interested in and motivated by good writing. It was tantalizing to envision publishing interestingly designed books, collaborative books, books with interior art.

What held us back? It was the obvious fact that both of us were working at more than full capacity to keep the journal alive and thriving. And yet the prospect of publishing books continued to allure us.

We eased into publishing books by sponsoring a competition we called Mountains in Minnesota, inviting collaborative chapbooks, a contest that received over sixty collaborative submissions and resulted in the publication of two small books in 1984: *Windy Tuesday Nights*, poems by Ralph Burns and evocative black-and-white landscapes by photographer Roger Pfingston, and *How We Missed Belgium*, a collaboration between two poets, Deborah Keenan and Jim Moore.

How We Missed Belgium was the beginning of our publication history with these two exceptional poets. In the years that followed, we published two award-winning, critically acclaimed titles by each of them: *The Freedom of History* and *The Long Experience of Love* by Jim Moore, and *Good Heart* and, after I left the press, *Willow Room, Green Door* by Deborah Keenan.

In 1984, we celebrated *Milkweed Chronicle*'s fourth year with the first Milkweed Editions book, an embodiment of our interest in combining art forms. *The Poet Dreaming in the Artist's House* was a collection of poems about the visual arts that I edited with poet Ruth Roston. Randy's art introduces each of the book's four parts, and his delicate drawings and engravings appear on most of the pages. I remember our pleasure and excitement when we opened a carton and paged through that first printed book. We sent *The Poet Dreaming in the Artist's House* to our subscribers as the Winter 1984 issue of *Milkweed Chronicle*.

The Journal—or Books

Because we were publishing books while we were still working on *Milkweed Chronicle*, the years from 1984 to 1987 were exceptionally hectic, so much so that our board members, more intelligent and practical than we were, insisted that we make a decision: publish the journal or publish books. We announced the decision to our readers as part of the preface to the final issue of *Milkweed Chronicle*.

Traveling On: Milkweed Editions

This is the last issue of the *Milkweed Chronicle*. To make this issue the last will enable us to commit our time and energy to acquiring, editing, designing, publishing, marketing, and distributing Milkweed Editions books.

This decision was not arrived at without considerable discussion. The *Chronicle* has been the focus of our attention for the past seven years. We've loved the work, experimenting with format, choosing each issue's content. We've had the satisfaction of printing fine work by a large number of writers and visual artists, and of being the first publication credit for many of them.

There is no "set" page of the *Chronicle*; the making of each issue is a hands-on, time-consuming process that involves counterpointing poems, juxtaposing words and images, and creating a visual flow throughout the issue that encourages browsing and then a reading and, we have hoped, a rereading. It's fun of the most satisfying kind; we will miss it very much.

We've been lucky in our readership. Many of you have been readers from our first years of publishing the *Chronicle*. You have stayed with us as we took up challenges of varying kinds: we have published three-hundred-line poems, changed from a tabloid format, presented unusual collaborations, added a separate cover, tried new papers and typefaces, and printed whole chapbooks in an issue. . . .

Since we began publishing books, we have found ourselves increasingly drawn by projects that we want to attempt, and by an ever-increasing number of book-length manuscripts we'd like to be able to publish. We've also found ourselves consistently behind the eight ball: understaffed and out of time. We knew that we had to make a choice. Fortunately, a small press is not a museum. The challenges change, the organization evolves.

We looked forward to our future in book publishing; nonetheless, we mourned the journal, especially because at the time we had no way of recording it, no way to invite readers to wander through its pages, a journey that would display the *Chronicle*'s true magic: expressive content embedded in a dynamic variety of visual formats, a combination of esthetic, emotional, and intellectual stimulation. I hope that future readers will be able to sample the journal electronically; at present, the issues exist only in the Milkweed Editions archives at the Elmer L. Andersen Library of the University of Minnesota.

Before I wrote this history, I reread every issue of *Milkweed Chronicle*, beginning with the forty-year-old inaugural issue. I wondered whether I'd find it stale, out-of-date, or irrelevant. I did not. As I dived into one issue after another, I was heartened to find them fresh and compelling, the writing emotionally alive and inviting. Ezra Pound was correct in at least one of his pronouncements: Poetry is news that stays news. I will add: Good writing will always be good reading.

Milkweed Editions Books: "Good Writing, Beautiful Books"

The transition from journal publishing to book publishing began in early 1985 with the publication of new books and a local distributor to help us get those books into bookstores. When the final issue of *Milkweed Chronicle* went to subscribers in 1987, we were already in the midst of publishing and marketing Milkweed Editions titles. Although we were newcomers to book publishing, we were not new to the authors, reviewers, bookstores, or funders in our community. We had forged affiliations, strengthened relationships, and made a surprising number of friends over the seven years we'd been around. What's more, we had a deep well of literary talent to draw from. Because we were already familiar with our writers and our audience, we had a head start as a book publisher.

We made a few basic decisions about our publishing agenda:

—We would continue the journal's tradition of welcoming new and emerging writers.
—We would look for manuscripts that married the allure of charged language with humane substance; we wanted to publish books that would be as relevant and rewarding to read in the future as on the day of their publication.
—We would build editorial time into each book we acquired to ensure that every book was at its best before we sent it into the world.
—We would maintain our emphasis on art and design. Each book would receive its own unique design and original cover art and, when appropriate, interior art as well.
—We would commit to keeping Milkweed titles in print for as long as possible instead of conforming to the industry practice of putting books out of print if they didn't sell well after the first year. That practice continues as part of the book industry's cycle of publishing seasons: New books are published each spring and fall, and many publishers also launch books in summer. New titles (the front list) receive extensive marketing and promotion, while older titles (the backlist) with fewer sales are often remaindered or pulped. Milkweed authors have often commented on the benefits of having their books available to readers for years after publication. In fact, the sales of some books increased after a few years as readers recommended them to friends.

Milkweed Editions—the First Books

Our early Milkweed Editions books grew out of relationships forged through the *Chronicle*; a majority of the books published during the 1980s were the works of Minnesota writers. The first titles we published were debut books of poetry by authors whose poems had previously appeared in the journal, each of them exceptional: Jill Breckenridge's *Civil Blood*; Jack Driscoll and Bill Meissner's collaboration, *Twin Sons of Different Mirrors*; Phebe Hanson's *Sacred Hearts*; Margaret Hasse's *In a Sheep's Eye, Darling*; Jim Moore's *The Freedom of History*; and Joe Paddock's *Earth Tongues*.

Our first translation was a book of poems, *Trusting Your Life to Water and Eternity*, by Norwegian poet Olav Hauge, translated by Robert Bly. We inaugurated the Thistle series, a collection of chapbook essays (small books on thorny subjects!), with Carol Bly's *Bad Government and Silly Literature* (a subject as relevant today as it was then), followed by David Mura's *A Male Grief: Notes on Pornography and Addiction*, and Judith Guest's *The Mythic Family*. We began mutually pleasurable relationships that continued well over twenty years with Minnesota writers Carol Bly, Bill Holm, and John Caddy.

Carol Bly was a formidable critic as well as a writer and a caring, exceptional teacher of writers, whose essays we published in *Milkweed Chronicle*. I admired her book *Letters from the Country*, essays about rural life, published in New York to national acclaim. I was just as enthusiastic about her short stories printed in regional magazines, especially "Gunnar's Sword," one of the finest short stories I've ever read. I asked Carol if Milkweed could bring out a collection of those short stories. When Carol's agent received a release from her New York publisher, we quickly moved ahead with *Backbone*. To our surprise and delight, the book received a glowing full-page review in the *New York Times Book Review*, generating our first significant sales.

During the next fifteen years, we published three additional titles with Carol: *The Passionate, Accurate Story: Making Your Heart's Truth into Literature* (1990), a book about how to turn one's deepest convictions into good writing; *Changing the Bully Who Rules the World: Reading and Thinking about Ethics* (1996), insights from literature and social work techniques to address aggression on every level of public and private life; and another collection of stories, *My Lord Bag of Rice: New and Selected Stories* (2000).

Bill Holm's *Boxelder Bug Variations: A Meditation on an Idea in Language and Music* was as unusual in its origin as in its contents. The journal's readership frequently commented favorably on Bill's wise, witty, antiauthoritarian essays and poems. One winter day, Bill drove from his home in western Minnesota across the state to Minneapolis to drop a four-hundred-page manuscript on my desk. He said, "This is a bunch of stuff about boxelder bugs. Is there a book in here somewhere?" There was.

Bill taught freshman English classes to deeply unappreciative college students in Marshall, Minnesota. He insisted that they could write about anything, anything at all, and make the subject fresh. When a boxelder bug marched across his desk, he told his students that their next assignment was to write about boxelder bugs, harmless but annoying insects that sheltered in midwestern houses and barns during the long winters. Bill went home and began to work on his own assignment.

With writer John Rezmerski, Bill's friend and colleague, I had the fun of extracting 102 pages of radium from the pitchblende of the original manuscript. The unique book that crawled out, in the words of a reviewer, "takes a seemingly common and small thing—the boxelder bug—and weaves a complex tapestry of musical, philosophical, political, and sociological meditations I never expected, including an explanation of the variation form, and of Bach's and Beethoven's contributions to the genre. In fact, this collection is basically Bill Holm's Goldberg Variations in words and music." Randy enriched and embellished the book with his own variations on boxelder tree leaves and bug motifs on every page.

Boxelder Bug Variations: A Meditation on an Idea in Language and Music was reprinted many times. Delighted readers let us know they treasured the book's originality, caustic wisdom, and humane insights. Readers today will find this book every bit as original and rewarding as did those who read it in 1985.

A year after the book's publication, we celebrated Bill's unique creation, as well as Phebe Hanson's *Sacred Hearts* and Joe Paddock's *Earth Tongues*, in the small town of Ghent in western Minnesota. I arrived by long-distance bus as the afternoon sky darkened and snow began to fall. Bill met me and took me to his home, a building whose excuse for being was to hold the books crammed into every nook of every room. When we arrived at the legion hall for the evening's pig roasting and poetry reading, the snow had become a blizzard. More than a hundred hardy Minnesotans came out of that raging snowstorm into the hall, stamping their boots and shaking snow off their hats and down jackets, to enjoy a companionable feast and an evening of poetry and music—and a beverage of choice. Bill wore a tuxedo for the occasion. Phebe and Joe and Bill read from their books, and then, on the resident venerable piano, Bill played some of the music and sang a few songs from *Boxelder Bug Variations*. No one left until we were told that the lights were about to be turned out.

Whenever I edited a book of Bill's, it was a pleasure that usually included more than one meeting over good food. Indeed, every one of his books includes recipes and allusions to splendid meals. Those books are: *Coming Home Crazy: An Alphabet of China Essays* (1990), a feast of a book about teaching in China; *The Heart Can Be Filled Anywhere on Earth* (1996), essays about Minneota, Minnesota; *The Dead Get By with Everything* (1991), which includes some of Bill's most haunting poems; *Eccentric Islands: Travels Real and Imaginary* (2000), about Bill's visits to island nations and those that existed only in his imagination or in favorite books; and a banquet of poetry, *Playing the Black Piano* (2004).

John Caddy's *Eating the Sting*, the winner of our Lake and Prairies Award for poetry in 1986, is a dazzling portrayal of the natural world he knew intimately from his upbringing in northern Minnesota. John's work as a poet and teacher reflected those years of wandering in the wild. During the 1960s and '70s, he taught writing in over eight hundred schools, with students ranging from kindergarten through graduate school.

In 1989, we published *The Color of Mesabi Bones*, John's emotionally charged poems drawn from his harsh childhood on Minnesota's iron range. No poet has done a better job of revealing what it is to be a young boy whose father bullies and terrorizes his family. The book received the prestigious Los Angeles Times Book Prize for poetry, given for the first time to a small press, as well as the Minnesota Book Award for poetry. That same year, John won the Poets & Writers Maureen Egen Writers Exchange Award and read at the Poetry Society of America in Manhattan, Los Angeles, and San Francisco.

Ten years later, John began writing a poem about the natural world every weekday morning and emailing it to subscribing classrooms in his Self-Expressing Earth (SEE) program at Hamline University's Center for Global Environmental Education. After the end of that program, he initiated a five-day-a-week program in 2001 called Morning Earth. First thing in the morning, John walked out into the woods around his home. When he came back, he wrote a poem about what struck his eye and emailed it (after 1995, the poem was accompanied by a photo) to thousands of readers. He considered his Morning Earth website, as he wrote, to be "an antidote to environmental despair, a resource toward ecoliteracy for teachers of students of all ages, and for everyone interested in the confluence of ecology and the arts." In 2003, Milkweed Editions published *Morning Earth: Field Notes in Poetry*, a collection of brief, enlivening poems with art by Randy Scholes, a small book that fit nicely into a hiker's backpack.

A Magnificent Outlier: Spillville

In 1985, Randy and I began work on *Spillville*, a project that had its roots in our enthusiasm for artists' books and the beauty of letterpress printing. *Spillville* is a collaboration between Patricia Hampl, who wrote the text, and Steven Sorman, who created the engravings, based on their journey with friends to Spillville, Iowa, the summer home, in 1893, of Czech composer Antonín Dvořák. Poet and essayist Patricia Hampl was the author of the celebrated memoir *A Romantic Education*. Artist Steven Sorman was well known for his mixed-media paintings, drawings, and prints in major national collections. Hampl's captivating story of their trip is a pilgrimage through a midwestern landscape, past and present, a meditation on art and beauty. Sorman's luminescent engravings provide a visual counterpoint to Hampl's text.

We resolved to honor this beautiful work by making the limited edition of *Spillville* an artist's book of the highest caliber. We collaborated with outstanding book artists at every step of the process to create 150 limited edition books. Sorman's twenty-seven engravings were printed on silky, semitranslucent, cream-colored Kitikata paper and then colléd (adhered) to heavyweight Grey Rives paper at Land Mark Editions in Minneapolis by master printers Bernice Ficek-Swenson, Jon Swenson, and Anya Szykitka.

The colléd pages were then delivered to master letterpress printer Norman Fritzberg at the Hansestadt Letterfoundry in St. Paul. He printed the text on each precious sheet of the Grey Rives paper next to Sorman's engravings. He used type cast for the book by Michael and Winifred Bixler of Skaneateles, New York, shipped by rail to St. Paul. Fritzberg himself specially cast the distinctive display type, Felix. Finally, he die-cut each page to size. The result was an exquisite loose-leaf book of forty-one individual pages combining text and image, placed unbound in a custom-made blue-cloth presentation box, with the title gold-stamped on the box.

The production of *Spillville* was an eye-opening experience. Shepherding text and art involved problem-solving by Randy at almost every step. Although the experts at each facility carried out the months of time-consuming labor with the greatest skill and care, Randy was involved far more than we anticipated. When the limited edition was completed, the result merited all the effort and care that went into its creation.

A full house of admirers attended the gala reading at the Walker Art Center in May 1987. From the stage, Patricia read the book aloud as pages of the limited edition were displayed on a large screen behind her.

The *Spillville* limited edition was hailed as an artistic triumph by the critical reviewers of *Fine Print*. Copies of the limited edition were purchased by major libraries and museums in the Twin Cities and around the country, and the work was chosen to be included in a traveling exhibit of the one hundred best American artists' books.

The reader's edition, adapted by Randy from the limited edition and published simultaneously, became our first of many 100 Notable Books of the Year designations from the *New York Times Book Review*. Louise Erdrich's comment sums up the critical response: "*Spillville* is a work of intense loveliness and lyrical magic, a splendid, difficult, and ultimately successful idea."

Milkweed kept the reader's edition of *Spillville* in print well into the twenty-first century; the limited edition continues to be available to viewers in libraries and museums, with a few copies still available for sale by Milkweed Editions. We concluded, with real regret, that because of cost and staff-time considerations, we couldn't continue to produce new limited editions and still fulfill our primary mission of publishing exceptional titles for a general audience. *Spillville* exists as a permanent treasure of book art, an artistic goal we were grateful to fulfill.

Milkweed Editions Fiction

1998 was the first year we awarded the Milkweed National Fiction Prize. Each year, the title that won the prize became a launching pad for that writer's literary career. The first winner was Arizona native Susan Lowell for *Ganado Red*. In the novella that accompanies this collection of stories, Lowell traces the ownership of an intricate Navajo rug, the Ganado red of the title, over sixty years, from its Navajo creator through its various owners. *Ganado Red* was named a Best Trade Paperback of the Year by *Publishers Weekly*.

In 1999, the winner was *Blue Taxis: Stories about Africa* by Eileen Drew, our second 100 Notable Books of the Year designation from the *New York Times Book Review*. The winner of the Milkweed

National Fiction Prize in 1990 was another debut, this one by author Susan Straight, for her collection of short fiction, *Aquaboogie*, named a Best Trade Paperback of the Year by *Publishers Weekly* and the winner of the Great Lakes Colleges Association New Writers Award. As a result of *Aquaboogie*'s critical success, Milkweed couldn't compete with the advances offered by mainstream presses for her next title. Nonetheless, we took real pleasure in knowing that Susan Straight's illustrious career as a novelist began its ascent with Milkweed Editions.

Bapsi Sidhwa's *Cracking India*, a book that had been rejected by a succession of mainstream publishers, won the Milkweed National Fiction Prize in 1991. *Cracking India* is a heart-wrenching novel about the 1947 partition of India. Lenny, the spirited child of a Parsee family living in the territory that became Pakistan, describes the era's horrific events; the reader learns of the religious zealotry and intolerance that resulted in a genocidal war whose reverberations continue to this day. *Cracking India* was designated a Notable Books of the Year by the *New York Times Book Review*; the winner of Germany's Liberatur Prize for Fiction; a New York Public Library Best Books for the Teen Age Award; and a Lila Wallace-Reader's Digest Writers' Award.

In an article about her work, Bapsi Sidhwa commented that the publication of *Cracking India* initiated the flood of fiction from New York publishers about the subcontinent. The novel was later made into a major motion picture, *Earth*, by acclaimed film artist Deepa Mehta. Our relationship with Bapsi continued with the publication of two endearing novels, *The Crow Eaters*, a vibrant window into life in India under British colonial rule, and *An American Brat*, an insightful and charming look at America from the perspective of a young Parsee girl visiting for the first time. In summing up Bapsi Sidhwa's work, the *New York Times* called her "Pakistan's finest English-language novelist."

From 1990 to 1992, Milkweed published award-winning fiction by authors Toni Ardizzone, Sandra Birdsell, Rosellen Brown, and

Marjorie Dorner. The 1992 winner of the Milkweed National Fiction Prize, *The Boy Without a Flag: Stories of the South Bronx*, by Abraham Rodriguez Jr., was a debut collection of realistic stories about the hard-edged lives of Puerto Rican teenagers coping with a culture that scorned and belittled them.

A Landmark Year

1993 was a year that changed Milkweed as an organization while also ushering in a period of remarkable progress in sales and national recognition.

Randy Scholes

Foremost among the changes that marked 1993 was one we deeply regretted: my fellow cofounder, Randy Scholes, decided that it was time for him to retire from Milkweed Editions to concentrate on his own artwork. His decision came after years without a vacation, years during which his workload dramatically increased while the pace of work continued to quicken.

At a special summer meeting of board and staff, Randy was celebrated for contributions impossible to overstate. After cofounding the press, Randy designed every issue of *Milkweed Chronicle*, creating original artwork for its pages. He designed every Milkweed Editions book. He crafted each cover, many of them original works of art based on the book's subject. Without his artistic brilliance, enthusiasm, and strong work ethic, there would have been no journal, nor without his partnership would I have felt encouraged to take on the challenge of starting a literary press.

Although Randy richly deserved the opportunity to concentrate on his own work as a designer and artist, we knew that we would miss not only his design skills and artwork but also his genial presence and contributions to our discussions and strategies. For Milkweed Editions, publishing without Randy would begin a new era of consulting with outside book designers and artists.

Montana 1948

Our new distributor assisted us in marketing a book that generated an entirely new level of sales. Larry Watson's *Montana 1948*, winner of the 1993 Milkweed National Fiction Prize, tells the story of the summer when a twelve-year-old boy's vision of his family's life is totally altered by events that involve his father, a small-town sheriff; his clear-sighted mother; his uncle, a doctor and war hero; and the family's Sioux housekeeper, whose disclosures are at the heart of the story. *Montana 1948* received a number of awards, including the American Library Association Booklist Editors' Choice Award as a Best Book of the Year, the Friends of American Writers Award for Best Fiction of the Year, and the Mountains & Plains Independent Booksellers Association Award for Best Fiction of the Year.

Montana 1948 sold more than thirty thousand hardcover books, a milestone for a press of our age and size. We licensed the paperback rights to Washington Square Press: their paperback edition sold well over one hundred twenty thousand copies—as heady for us as it was for Larry Watson. A few years later we published Larry's novel *Justice*, another distinctive literary western, to additional acclaim and very respectable sales. These two titles marked the resurgence of Larry Watson's literary career, which continues to flourish.

Fiction through 2000

Our fiction program moved from strength to strength with the publication of William Carpenter's *A Keeper of Sheep*, described by the *New Yorker* as "prose that manages to be unobtrusive and gorgeous at the same time," and *Swimming in the Congo* by Margaret Meyers, whose brilliant collection of stories about Africa was characterized as "*Anne of Green Gables* meets *Heart of Darkness*." Two years later, we published Tessa Bridal's *The Tree of Red Stars*, a novel about a young woman combatting a fascist regime in Uruguay that has been translated into five languages and named the winner of the Friends of American Writers Award for Best Fiction of the Year. British writer Lee Langley's *Persistent Rumours*, winner of England's Writers' Guild/Macallan

Award for Best Novel, was described in the *Daily Mail* as "The closest thing to a faultless novel I have read for years. . . . Lee Langley shows that the effort to understand the past is never wasted."

In the mid-1990s, we published three accomplished, innovative novels by David Haynes. The first of these, *Somebody Else's Mama*, is a moving portrait of an African American family with a memorable mother-in-law. The *New York Times Book Review* commented that "Miss Keezie has the old-time strength of Eudora Welty's Phoenix Jackson. . . . It is her voice, demonstrating Mr. Haynes's flawless ear, that makes his novel come to life." After the publication of *Somebody Else's Mama*, Haynes was selected as one of *Granta*'s Best Young American Novelists and received the Friends of American Writers Award for Adult Literature. Milkweed's next Haynes novel, *Live at Five*, described as "touching and wickedly funny" by *Publishers Weekly*, features a TV newscaster whose producer decides that his middle-class African American commentator isn't "black" enough. *Essence* describes his third novel, *All American Dream Dolls*, a book that added to Haynes's growing reputation as a writer of distinction, as "a wildly funny look at a Black woman's life."

When novelist Faith Sullivan, author of the bestselling novel *The Cape Ann*, asked Bill Holm to recommend a publisher for her next title, he suggested that Milkweed Editions might be the right home for her future books. Bill's suggestion led to a harmonious relationship with Faith that resulted in Milkweed's publication of her Harvester, Minnesota, novels, beginning in 1996 with the highly praised *The Empress of One*, followed in 2000 by *What a Woman Must Do*.

Part of the pleasure of my job was scouting journals in search of literary talent. In 1988, I read a story that I found so innovative and appealing, I decided to call the writer long-distance. It was a much longer distance than I had anticipated. I woke Ken Kalfus out of a sound sleep in Moscow, half a world away. I agreed to call back the next day. With the acquisition of his collection of extraordinarily inventive stories, *Thirst*, we became writer Ken Kalfus's first publisher. Critic Dwight Garner wrote: "The thirteen stories in *Thirst* work something like poison; you touch them to your lips, and you're instantly seduced. You plunge in for the duration." The following year, Ken's dazzling and varied tales of old and new Russia in *Pu-239 and Other Russian Fantasies* brought him additional national huzzahs, including the Independent Publisher Book Awards Editor's Choice Award and repeat *New York Times Book Review* and *Philadelphia Inquirer* Notable Book of the Year designations.

A New Genre: Books for Young Readers

The Books for Young Readers program, books for nine-to-twelve-year-olds, came about in response to mainstream publishers' concentration on acquiring best-selling series like *Goosebumps* and *Sweet Valley High*, a trend that led to a drastic reduction in the publishing of individual novels for intermediate-age readers.

Susan Lowell, the author of *Ganado Red*, was the author of Milkweed's first title for young readers, *I Am Lavina Cumming*, about growing up in the early years of the American West; the book received the Mountains & Plains Independent Booksellers Association Regional Book Award, as well as the Arizona Library Association's Children's Author Award. For the next twelve years we published distinctive, well-reviewed novels for young readers that appealed to many thousands. *Behind the Bedroom Wall* by Laura E. Williams, a Maud Hart Lovelace Book Award finalist and a Jane Addams Children's Book Honor Award winner, sold more than 130,000 copies.

Stories from Where We Live

We added significantly to the young readers program with the *Stories from Where We Live* series. Author and editor Sara St. Antoine contacted me about initiating a series of children's books that would describe the natural history of each of the different North American ecoregions with literature appropriate for kids ages nine and up. St. Antoine spoke of these books as literary field guides—stories, poems, journals, and essays that showed the lives of people in a geographical area, as well as the animals, plants, weather, and landscapes that made the region unique. We welcomed St. Antoine's vision as a perfect addition not only to our children's literature program but also to our Literature for a Land Ethic program. Trudy Nicholson's beautiful black-and-white illustrations are featured throughout the books, while artist Paul Mirocha's distinctive maps serve as covers for each title.

In 2000 we published the first volume of *Stories from Where We Live—The North Atlantic Coast: A Literary Field Guide.* In the next few years, we added these to the series: *The Great Lakes, The South Atlantic Coast and Piedmont, The Great North American Prairie, The Gulf Coast,* and *The California Coast.* The journal *Book Report* commented: "This series is sure to be a hit with classes studying the regional geography of the United States, and it would be a superb resource for classes and teaching teams that integrate language and social studies."

Nonfiction in the Public Interest

We returned to the title of the editorial in the first issue of *Milkweed Chronicle, Where Do We Come From? What Are We? Where Are We Going?*—a title drawn from the magnificent Gauguin canvas on which those questions are painted—in 1992, during a long-range planning process we completed with our board, asking ourselves those vital questions once again. We discussed our past work, and, at some of our liveliest meetings, enriched by the comments of advisors from bookselling and publishing, we talked about the future of literary publishing and the role of Milkweed Editions. We talked about the great privilege of being able to connect writers and readers in a communion of ideas and values, including the shared belief that literature has the power to change the way we look at the world, the power to change ideas, to change lives, and thus to make a humane impact on society. As a result of that planning process, we made the decision to concentrate Milkweed's nonfiction titles in areas of ethical, cultural, and environmental interest. With the encouragement and endorsement of our board of directors, we crafted a new mission to publish more books that embodied this transformative power, and to continue to publish them beautifully:

> Milkweed Editions publishes with the intention of making a humane impact on society, in the belief that literature is a transformative art uniquely able to convey the essential experiences of the human heart and spirit. To that end, Milkweed Editions publishes distinctive voices of literary merit in handsomely designed, visually dynamic books, exploring the ethical, cultural, and esthetic issues that free societies need continually to address.

From that time forward, every book we considered for publication was vetted on the basis of whether it contributed to fulfilling that mission.

Nonfiction

We began our nonfiction initiative by focusing on a pervasive social justice issue that touched the lives of millions: sexual violence against women. In late 1992, in the aftermath of a brutal rape and murder of a young woman in northern Minnesota, I looked through the literature on the subject, and I found surprisingly little about *preventing* sexual violence. I invited two academic colleagues, Martha Roth and Pamela Fletcher, to join me as coeditors of *Transforming a Rape Culture*, a book intended to address the persistence as well as the extent of sexual violence against women. Our intention was to change the status quo by examining the subject from a cultural perspective. We spent six months reading every book published about rape and found that every one of those books was written from the perspective of the survivors, none of whom had been accorded justice. We found it disturbing that there was no broad overview of this major social catastrophe.

We brought together focus groups of women and mixed-gender focus groups and listened to their opinions and suggestions. We found an expert in each cultural arena to write an essay for the book. The diverse contributors, female and male, were activists, opinion leaders, theologians, policy makers, and educators. If a potent essay on a particular subject already existed, we asked for permission to include it.

The pioneering anthology we published in 1993 was intended to call attention to the need for fundamental cultural change, no less than the transformation of basic attitudes about power, gender, race, and sexuality.

The first section of *Transforming a Rape Culture* offers statistical evidence of the fact that rape is part of a continuum of sexual violence in American culture, documenting the fact that every facet of our society abets sexual violence, including the differing education of boys and girls, the culture of violence in sports, the ubiquitous impact of pornography, the commodification of women, the emphasis in most religions on women's submission to men, and the language surrounding sexuality. The next two sections depict strategies for change, including examples of activism, a roadmap for forward movement, and successful programs for implementing that change. The final section of the book looks to the future, presenting visions of and possibilities for a sexual-violence-free culture.

We kicked off publication with a reading to an enthusiastic audience at St. Catherine University in St. Paul, the first of many readings at colleges around the country. We were encouraged by the positive reviews and by the fact that the *New York Times Book Review* chose the book as a Notable Book of the Year. *Transforming a Rape Culture* was adopted as required reading by colleges for courses in a variety of disciplines. In 2003, we published a second edition of the book, updating the statistics and removing some essays while adding eight new ones on the topics of the Internet, the role of sports in abetting sexual violence, and rape as a calculated instrument of war.

The topics we explored in these two editions continue to be at the forefront of the national debate about sexual violence. Recently, the necessity to shelter at home during the COVID-19 pandemic fueled a resurgence of domestic violence. Because social change is a notoriously and dishearteningly slow process, sexual violence against women—and men—will continue to require ongoing conversation, debate, and political activism.

A book that speaks both to cultural norms and to ethical possibilities, Carol Bly's *Changing the Bully Who Rules the World: Reading and Thinking about Ethics* is a bracing commentary about culture and ethics. Bly, a promoter of cooperation between teachers and social workers, argues that we haven't used our knowledge of social psychology or the riches of literature for reconceptualizing and understanding our lives. Anyone—an employer, a partner, a business, the government—can become the bully or bullies in our lives and in the lives of others. *Changing the Bully Who Rules the World* presents hopeful, practical ideas intended to hasten ethical change both in thinking and in behavior, with excerpts from exceptional literature, including the voices of Charles Baxter, Donald Hall, Jim Harrison, Mark Helprin, Denise Levertov, Thomas McGrath, Joyce Carol Oates, Mary Oliver, Katha Pollitt, Alice Walker, Tobias Wolff, and others.

Mary Rose O'Reilley's ethical and spiritual autobiography, *The Barn at the End of the World: The Apprenticeship of a Quaker, Buddhist Shepherd*, is a superlative read. Deciding that her life was insufficiently grounded in real-world experience, O'Reilley, a Quaker reared as a Catholic, embarked on a year of tending sheep. In this entertaining and frequently hilarious book, O'Reilley describes a year of learning to care for sheep, followed by an extended visit to a Buddhist monastery in France, where she absorbs the teachings of Thich Nhat Hanh and the practice of Mahayana Buddhism. She seeks as well as transmits from both barn and monastery a spirituality based not in "climbing out of the body" but rather in existing fully in the world.

The World As Home Program: Literary Nonfiction about the Natural World

In the mid-1990s, to increase public awareness of the increasing challenges to the natural world, we refocused our nonfiction program to feature books about environmental stewardship. When Bill Holm heard that author Paul Gruchow was looking for a publisher for his new book about Minnesota' s failing rural environment, he sent Paul to Milkweed Editions. Our mutual commitment to these issues led to a friendship and to the publication of Gruchow's beloved titles, beginning with *Grass Roots: The Universe of Home*. That marvelous book issues a powerful warning against corporate agriculture. Gruchow describes how difficult it had become for farmers to continue to make their livelihood on the land and to maintain rural community. Over the course of fifty years, farms had been swept away by large commercial entities with no interest in or connection to the land. Rural children had grown up in a world that rejected the contributions of their parents and grandparents.

Gruchow begins *Grass Roots* with a question and a comment that resonates through the best writing about our relationship with the natural world:

> What if one's life were not a commodity, not something to be bartered to the highest bidder, or made to order? What if one's life were governed by needs more fundamental than acceptance or admiration? What if one were simply to stay home and plant some manner of garden? To plant a garden is to enter the continuum of time. Each seed carries in its genome the history that will propel it into the future, and in planting it we stretch one of the long threads of our culture into tomorrow.

A few years later, Milkweed published Paul Gruchow's *Boundary Waters: The Grace of the Wild*, in which Gruchow skis, backpacks, and canoes through the Boundary Waters, turning his naturalist's eye on a wilderness of wolves, moose, bears, and loons, contemplating the richness of this natural heritage. In 1999 we reprinted Gruchow's *The Necessity of Empty Places*, meditations on the "empty" places that offer solace—grasslands, deserts, river shallows—often bypassed by tourists looking for more spectacular views. Taken together, these books are a legacy of wisdom about the crucial need to maintain natural treasures in the face of exploitation.

Author Annick Smith's devotion to the land she loves shines throughout *Homestead*, a generous memoir that traces more than thirty years of her life spent on Montana ranchland, in the not-so-distant West of outlaws and pioneers, range inspectors and cattle thieves, while she made a new life for her sons after the tragic, early death of her husband.

In 1995 I received an SOS from writer and earth defender Terry Tempest Williams: Utah wilderness was under siege. She and author Stephen Trimble were fighting to protect public Utah land being bought up by private industry. At the same time, they were attempting, with their congressman, to pass a bill in Congress that would make the land a national monument. Essays by distinguished writer friends, including William Kittredge, Barry Lopez, John McPhee, Mark Strand, Ann Haymond Zwinger, and fifteen other prominent novelists, nature writers, and poets, were gathered into a book as testimony about the need to protect and preserve America's wilderness habitats.

Terry asked Milkweed to *quickly* publish *Testimony: Writers of the West Speak On Behalf of Utah Wilderness*, which we did. Terry and Stephen took the newly printed books to Washington, DC, to support the bill. They placed a copy of *Testimony* on the desk of every single congressperson. The next afternoon Terry called to let us know that the bill establishing the Grand Staircase-Escalante National Monument and protecting a million acres of wild land, had passed.

On September 18, 1996, President Bill Clinton held a copy of *Testimony* in his hands on the rim of the Grand Canyon as he proclaimed the new Grand Staircase-Escalante National Monument.

Robert Redford invited the *Testimony* contributors, and three of us from Milkweed, to celebrate the first public reading of the book at Sundance. It was a rare opportunity to witness the power of literature in creating public policy.

In 1999, we formalized "The World As Home" as the title that encompassed Milkweed's publishing program dedicated to exploring the human relationship with the natural world and the environment. Some of our fiction, poetry, and children's titles augmented our environmental stewardship agenda.

We launched the World As Home website the following year as a resource for educators, writers, activists—everyone interested in nature writing as a source of ecological literacy and renewal. We believed that literary writing about the natural world could become a key source of knowledge and understanding in bringing natural places to life in the minds of readers. We invited educators to consider using the books for their classes, offering discounts to schools, libraries, and institutional accounts. The main feature of the site was a map of fifteen ecoregions covering much of North America. Clicking through the map brought up online resources of literary writing about the natural world, including information about organizations dedicated to protecting their ecoregions and information about endangered landscapes. The site's homepage featured a new theme every week.

We commissioned the Credo series—books by writers chosen by series editor Scott Slovic for their commitment to preserving the natural world. At the time, Scott was a professor of literature and environment at the University of Nevada, the editor of the leading journal about that subject, and the founding president of the Association for the Study of Literature and Environment.

The writers in the Credo series spoke from their hearts as well as from their extensive knowledge. Each writer was asked to express his or her credo of core beliefs about the natural world and the human community, describing essential goals, concerns, and practices. Each volume is the writer's investigation of what it means to present human experience in the context of the more-than-human world. Each book includes a biographical profile and a complete bibliography of the author's published works. Over six years, these books of personal reflection and insight by some of America's pre-eminent environmental writers joined the Credo series:

Rick Bass, *Brown Dog of the Yaak: Essays on Art and Activism* (1999)

Pattiann Rogers, *The Dream of the Marsh Wren: Writing As Reciprocal Creation* (1999)

William Kittredge, *Taking Care: Thoughts on Storytelling and Belief* (1999)

Scott Russell Sanders, *The Country of Language* (1999)

Robert Michael Pyle, *Walking the High Ridge: Life As Field Trip* (2000)

Ann Haymond Zwinger, *Shaped by Wind and Water: Reflections of a Naturalist* (2000)

Alison Hawthorne Deming, *Writing the Sacred into the Real* (2001)

John Elder, *The Frog Run: Words and Wildness in the Vermont Woods* (2001)

John Nichols, *An American Child Supreme: The Education of a Liberation Ecologist* (2001)

John Daniel, *Winter Creek: One Writer's Natural History* (2002)

Gary Paul Nabhan, *Cross-Pollinations: The Marriage of Science and Poetry* (2004)

Joseph Bruchac, *At the End of Ridge Road* (2005)

After our energizing involvement with *Testimony*, we continued harnessing the power of outstanding nature writing in a two-pronged approach: publishing nonfiction anthologies we called Literature for the Land, collections about nature writing and areas of environmental concern; and titles by individual nature writers about their relationships with animals and land.

By 2003 we had published the following anthologies in the Literature for the Land series: *This Incomparable Land: A Guide to American Nature Writing*, edited by Thomas J. Lyon; *Wild Earth:*

Wild Ideas for a World Out of Balance, edited by Tom Butler; *The Book of the Tongass*, edited by Carolyn Servid and Donald Snow; *The Book of the Everglades*, edited by Susan Cerulean; and *The Colors of Nature: Culture, Identity, and the Natural World*, by Alison Deming and Lauret Savoy.

The titles by individual nature writers were intended to reach a wide audience interested in memoir and personal interactions with nature. They included: *On Landscape and Longing*, by Carolyn Servid; *Swimming with Giants: My Encounters with Whales, Dolphins, and Seals*, by Anne Collet; *A Wing in the Door: Life with a Red-Tailed Hawk*, by Peri Phillips McQuay; *The Prairie in Her Eyes*, by Ann Daum; *A Sense of the Morning: Field Notes of a Born Observer*, by David Brendan Hopes; and *The Pine Island Paradox: Making Connections in a Disconnected World*, by Kathleen Dean Moore.

When we received the manuscript of *Ecology of a Cracker Childhood* by author, naturalist, and activist Janisse Ray, Janisse and I spent hours on the phone talking about the fact that mainstream publishers wanted to publish her work if they could keep the part of her story about growing up impoverished and regulated by rigid fundamentalism in her father's junkyard, but eliminate her passionate description of the almost-vanished longleaf pine ecosystem that once covered millions of acres across the South. This destruction is emblematic of the ongoing commercial efforts to deforest, defoliate, and destroy the natural world in pursuit of profit while disregarding long-term sustainability. We told Janisse that we admired the book as a whole, a lived experience that captured her love of the land where she grew up. Janisse's book received superlative reviews on publication and in a few years the book was viewed as a classic of American nature writing.

The *Testimony* model of protest against commercial incursions on vulnerable lands and waters continued to be influential. In 2001, Alaska residents Hank Lentfer and Carolyn Servid responded to proposals to drill in the Arctic National Wildlife Refuge by sending out a call to writers across the country. The result was *Arctic Refuge: A Circle of Testimony*, presented to Congress with testimonies by Rick Bass, Wendell Berry, President Jimmy Carter, Barry Lopez, Bill

McKibben, Scott Russell Sanders, and Terry Tempest Williams. *Arctic Refuge* introduced both the uniqueness of the Arctic Refuge and the issues surrounding energy use and the despoiling of public lands. Unfortunately, to this day, the corporations that hope to extract oil and minerals in this fragile environment continue to press their claims to invade and despoil the Arctic National Wildlife Refuge.

In April of 2021, I learned from Scott Slovic, now a professor of literature and environment at the University of Idaho, that he has taught *Testimony*-model workshops in many different cities around the world, from Madrid to Shanghai to Islamabad, and has lectured on the tradition of wilderness-testimony collections. He comments that in recent decades he has seen international interest increase in creating these testimonies to beloved landscapes. I find it exhilarating that this movement to preserve precious habitat has gained worldwide momentum. Literature is playing a significant role in engaging the hearts and minds of readers in efforts to preserve and honor the planet we have been desecrating and whose sentient life we have been harrying toward extinction. This literature of hope and commitment needs to multiply.

The Mission of a Nonprofit Press

Commercial publishers are under constant pressure to maximize profitability. Thus, before a book is acquired by a mainstream press, it is scrutinized for sales potential. "How many copies will this book sell?" is a valid question for a commercial press to ask when making an acquisition. Milkweed's status as a nonprofit press allows us the privilege of acquiring a book without regard for its sales potential but rather because it fulfills our mission.

A nonprofit press has the opportunity, indeed, the obligation, to take the time necessary to bring a manuscript to its fullest life. As examples of what a mission-driven nonprofit press can do supremely well—that is, provide unique and valuable experiences for readers and nurture the work of emerging writers to grow into its full potential—I'll cite two books I edited toward the end of my years at

Milkweed: *Song of the World Becoming: New and Collected Poems, 1981–2001* by Pattiann Rogers and *Ordinary Wolves* by Seth Kantner.

We were elated that in 2000, Milkweed Editions could take on the responsibility of publishing a 518-page hardcover edition of a book of poetry. *Song of the World Becoming: New and Collected Poems, 1981–2001* by Pattiann Rogers is a major contribution to American letters. Such a large book of poetry requires scrupulous copyediting as well as indexing. Such a book is expensive to typeset and print, and there is no guarantee that the costs to produce the book will be recouped by sales. The comments we received from writers about the book were unabashedly rhapsodic. Barry Lopez wrote: "If angels were to agree upon a language to describe creation, a tone of voice and a point of view that would adequately celebrate the divine, these would be the poems they would write. . . . If this is not poetry in service to humanity, I do not know what is." Diane Ackerman wrote: "A brilliant onrushing voice pours evenly throughout her poems, as if they were a single reverent song of life. . . . Having so many gathered together in one volume is a long-awaited pleasure." Scott Russell Sanders commented: "Here is a wealth of hard, loving, precise thought about the universe and its creatures unrivaled by any poet in our time." The union of scientific and poetic insights Rogers brings to her view of the universe and the variety of its creations is a hallelujah of praise and wonder, a celebration of the other living beings with whom we share the planet. Publishing this book was an achievement we treasured.

In 1999, a respected literary agent unexpectedly sent me a package containing a letter and a bulky manuscript by an unpublished writer. The letter explained that the manuscript had been rejected by a number of mainstream publishers. Even so, the agent wrote, she hoped that we would take into account the talent of the writer as well as the unusual subject matter and consider the book for publication. That afternoon I sat down at my desk to glance at the manuscript. I found myself transported into the world of a young American boy who wanted to be an Inupiat hunter, living in a sod igloo in the frozen wilderness of remotest northwestern Alaska. I entered an elemental world of wolves and moose, of sled dogs and subsistence hunters and trappers living on the tundra, a brilliant story of anger and despair in response to the desecration of wilderness. When I looked up, hours later, I knew why the agent hadn't given up on this writer. Seth Kantner's every sentence shimmered with fresh detail, bringing the wide, wild, snow-blown tundra landscape and its people and animals to vivid life. I realized that trekking through the wilderness of a five-hundred-page manuscript overwhelmingly in need of reorganization would mean spending many months working with the author. Of course we accepted the manuscript.

Seth Kantner and I entered into an author-editor relationship of almost four years, the process curtailed by the fact that for six months of the year, Seth was off the grid, hunting, trapping, fishing, and trading, earning money in places where there was no reception by phone. When Seth returned from earning a living, we exchanged sections of the manuscript, spoke on the phone, and wrestled with decisions, including ultimately jettisoning a tangential section of the manuscript. Eventually the manuscript become *Ordinary Wolves*. *Publishers Weekly* gave it a starred review, describing it as "a riveting first novel [that] sets a new standard. . . . A *tour de force* and maybe the best treatment of the Northwest and its people since Jack London's works." The *New York Times Book Review* praised it as "a magnificently realized story." Louise Erdrich wrote, "I've not read anything that so captures the contrast between the wild world and our ravaging consumer culture. *Ordinary Wolves* is painful and beautiful." Seth Kantner's agent was absolutely right to champion his work, and we were fortunate that our priorities as a press allowed us to give this fierce and astonishing book the gestation time it needed. These two books, *Ordinary Wolves* and *Song of the World Becoming: New and Collected Poems, 1981–2001*, also added a dimension of potent fiction and poetry to Milkweed's World As Home program.

Milkweed's Board of Directors

From the outset, board members were essential contributors to the press. When Randy and I started *Milkweed Chronicle*, the two of us and four benevolent board members kept our enterprise afloat. We added to our board before we could afford even part-time staff, and therefore the input of the board was vital to Milkweed as Randy and I learned the ropes. A few years later, the board inaugurated committees—governance, finance, development, marketing, education, and administration—that generated reports to assist us in achieving our objectives and garnering funding support. Each board member agreed to serve for a three-year term, renewable for another three years. With only one or two exceptions, Milkweed board members elected to stay on for the full six-year period. Additionally, board members willingly took part in lengthy strategic retreats as part of prestigious advancement and challenge grants from the National Endowment for the Arts.

Each of our board chairs (bless them!) willingly took on time-consuming tasks and responsibilities, including fundraising as well as consulting on potentially difficult issues. The head of the finance committee served as a source of advice and sound judgment in those years before we had a financial director on staff. Until we had a fairly steady income stream from sales, our finances were dependent on major grants being approved before others were depleted, a circumstance not unusual for small nonprofits. There were more than a few nights when I paced the living room worrying about cash flow and meeting payroll. Through the periods of financial ups and downs, the board's experience and active assistance helped us stay in the black. Like other small arts groups, we had no financial cushion to fall back on, a situation that would be remedied only many years later when we were able to raise capital in a cash reserve for such occasions.

Individual members came up with a variety of helpful ideas and solutions. For example, a board member from the finance committee accompanied me to meetings with the interviewing member of a funding organization to answer questions about our resources and stability. A member of the development committee came up with a creative idea for our yearly fundraiser; she organized a "friends of" group that staffed the first and subsequent Book Lovers Balls, and as a result, her friends became our friends. A governance committee member held evening gatherings of acquaintances at his home, offering an opportunity for me to talk to the group about our mission and our books. Those evening get-togethers convinced some of the guests that Milkweed was worth their support. Board members bought copies of Milkweed books as gifts, expanding our readership.

In summary, board members were not only the custodians of our mission but also its supportive emissaries. They helped us through the rough spots. They cheered us on. They rejoiced when Milkweed achieved a milestone. They celebrated our literary breakthroughs and triumphs. We certainly would not have survived to achieve eventual recognition and success without their assistance and support.

Milkweed Staff

As I discovered at Milkweed, the staff of a literary press is its secret treasure. Each staff member is an individual who enjoys reading books as well as the process of making books and marketing them. Each staff member is committed to the work, aware of the importance of his or her role.

As I mentioned earlier, we added our first two full-time hires in 1986. What a difference it made to be joined by two highly effective, high-spirited book people! During their tenure we were able to boost our outreach materially, sending out our first catalogs and other marketing materials. At that time, we received our first National Endowment for the Arts grant, the beginning of consistent national support. By 1991, our budget could sustain a staff of seven; for the next few years, depending on funding, staff members numbered six or seven. We added our first full-time financial director in 1993. A year later, we engaged a discerning critic and reviewer as our freelance first reader and editorial consultant. In 1995, we hired our first full-time marketing director, managing editor, office manager, and our first full-time editorial and marketing assistants. From that time forward, we were a staff of between nine and eleven, with an intensive internship program, equipped with the person-power to execute thoroughly in every area of our publishing.

We had the usual weekly staff meetings to update and inform, but we also gathered staff for impromptu meetings to collect responses to cover mock-ups for new titles or to gauge opinions about marketing ideas. We were a convivial group, celebrating birthdays over leisurely lunch excursions. The office atmosphere was relaxed and lighthearted, but the work we did together was exemplary and thoroughly professional. We had the time to get to know and value one another. It was a pleasure to make books with exceptional and dedicated coworkers.

Our Offices: Open Book

For the first twelve years, our home base was the Hennepin Center for the Arts in downtown Minneapolis; we moved offices three times within that building, each time in need of more space. Due to rent increases, we looked for other quarters and, in 1994, found space only a block away, at 430 First Avenue North. But soon enough, there was a rent increase, and then another, a common problem for nonprofit arts organizations. After an initial meeting between Linda Myers, the executive director of the Loft, and Jay Cowles, the president of the board of directors of the Minnesota Center for Book Arts, about the ongoing office-space problem, the discussion expanded to include Peggy Korsmo-Kennon, MCBA's executive director, and me. The board and staff of our three organizations launched a joint effort to come up with solutions. We received planning funds to investigate options for a common home with a stable rent.

In 1998, we decided that the best solution for all of us was to purchase a building. The group created a nonprofit corporation, Minnesota Open Book and Literary Building Inc. In November of that year, the corporation bought three conjoined nineteenth-century buildings on Washington Avenue in need of radical surgery. Spearheaded by the spirited engagement of Jay Cowles and MCBA board member Chris Mahai, and joined by board members of all three organizations, the corporation held a successful campaign that raised over seven million dollars to renovate the buildings into a new entity that would house all of us: Milkweed, the Loft, and MCBA. Garth Rockcastle of MSR Design was chosen as the architect. Garth met regularly with a planning committee from our three groups to ensure that each of our space needs would be met. As the restoration work approached conclusion, Sid Farrar, Milkweed's executive director at the time, had already received one temporary lease extension for Milkweed, but the landlord was not willing to grant a second. With Milkweed's lease expiring in a matter of weeks, Open Book provided funds from the campaign so that we could move from our offices on the fourth floor of our building to a temporary space on the sixth floor. Sid commented, "We were in this horrible space for nearly a year. It had no windows, and we were crammed in. The heating system was very bad. We found out that one of our upstairs neighbors was a gold-plating business. At regular intervals they would start grinding, and it sounded like a bowling ball rolling across the floor."

Our holding pattern ended on February 26, 2000, when the Milkweed crew moved into our new quarters on the third floor of Open Book. The building's elevator was still being installed, but we decided to go ahead with the move. We watched with excitement and some anxiety as a crane moved furniture up into our offices through a window.

We walked up the two flights of stairs into our light-filled spaces, marveling that the years of preparation were over. We were at home. In the next weeks, the Loft and MCBA were settled on the floors below us. This inspiring collaboration among nonprofits succeeded because of the tremendous support we received from board members, from individual donors, and from most of the Twin Cities funding community. In the auditorium of our new building, Milkweed could host publication readings and events such as our annual fundraiser, the Book Lovers Ball, a festive evening of readings. Open Book was the first building in the country to house collaborating literary nonprofit organizations; the building was a source of pride for the Twin Cities and served as a model for other communities. Since it opened to the public, Open Book has been a place for visitors and tenants alike to enjoy, whether relaxing over coffee and snacks at the café, attending classes at the Loft or at MCBA, or, for those of us on the third floor, creating new books.

From Milkweed's Past to the Milkweed Editions of Today

One afternoon years ago, long before I retired, I was in New York visiting a reviewer to talk about the next season of Milkweed titles. On my way down, the elevator stopped to admit a woman and a man talking animatedly about the number of "units" they expected to place during the next month and the total "units" they believed that they could sell through that year. It took me a few moments to realize that the *units* they were talking about were not bars of soap or boxes of cereal. They were talking about *books*. I had never before thought of books in terms of units, but here, in one of the hubs of the book industry, I was listening to everyday book business talk. I was reminded that the goals of industrial publishing have always been and continue to be maximum profitability and market domination through volume. Mergers in the publishing industry continue today, as it contracts yet again from six enormous entities to three multibillion dollar publishing Goliaths.

Like most booklovers, I believe that each book is as individual as a fingerprint, each a unique creation. A civilization is known by its arts, among them, books. Literary books expand the sense of what is possible, what is meaningful, what is ethical. The books we cherish and take to heart are more than a mirror of who we are—they play a role in shaping us, forming our identity as individuals and as societies. I believe that literary books benefit from the existence of a humanistic model of publishing, a mode represented by nonprofit literary presses that encourage and promote new and emerging writers, publishing books that broaden, deepen, and enliven the culture. That model, an alternative to the industrial publishing culture that commands today's mainstream publishing, is represented by today's Milkweed Editions, a prime example of a humanist literary nonprofit publisher. The press I was privileged to shepherd for twenty-four years has grown and matured, significantly increasing its book publications and publishing program. Milkweed has enlarged and broadened the scope of its thriving poetry program as well as its literary nonfiction celebrating the natural world and protecting the environment. Active publishing in the ebook and audiobook markets has, along with growing foreign rights sales, expanded the audience for Milkweed books, giving the press a more global presence.

Remarkably, Milkweed Editions has quintupled its sales over the past five years. In late 2020, the press had two books on the *New York Times* nonfiction best-seller list for several weeks. During the same period, Milkweed had a National Book Award finalist, two Pulitzer Prize finalists, and a National Book Critics Circle Award winner in poetry.

I applaud the growing Seedbank publishing initiative, world literature that brings ancient, historical, and contemporary works from a multiplicity of cultures to American readers, conveying insights into endangered or forgotten ways of seeing the world. Another innovation I admire in today's Milkweed is the presence of the Milkweed Bookstore on the ground floor of Open Book, stocked with high-quality literary books from a plethora of publishers, a splendid place to browse.

Milkweed's humanist agenda grew organizationally as well. The press replaced its internship program with a salaried fellowship program. With an intentional outreach to communities long underrepresented in the publishing industry, this program has enabled Milkweed to accomplish the related objectives of offering excellent employment opportunities to people of color, diversifying the staff, enriching the range of perspectives in the process, and, it is to be hoped, preparing fellows to continue on to paid employment, eventually to assume leadership positions in publishing.

As the press celebrates more than forty continuous years of publishing—no mean feat!—today's Milkweed Editions is flourishing and ascendant after sixteen years of outstanding leadership by publisher Daniel Slager.

Moving On

Once we settled into Open Book, the press entered a period of as much stability as any literary nonprofit press might reasonably expect. Therefore, I was surprised to find myself thinking about retiring. There was no particular reason for these thoughts; on the contrary, I thoroughly enjoyed every aspect of my job, treasure hunting through manuscripts to find life-enhancing writing, working with writers, being involved in the design process for new titles, and promoting Milkweed when I spoke at meetings and at writers' conferences. And yet I had begun to think about what it would be like, after almost a quarter of a century, to spend more of my life with our grown family, to write, to read indiscriminately, or simply to do nothing if I felt like it. It occurred to me that retirement had moved to the forefront of my thoughts, because I realized that the press was as secure and as well positioned for the future as any nonprofit literary press could be. Milkweed Editions was a known entity, a leading national literary press, fiscally stable, with a stellar staff and board. I could, if I wished, retire, confident that the press would continue to thrive.

In 2002, I made the bittersweet decision. I told the board that I intended to leave the following year, when I turned sixty-eight. I asked them to begin a search for the best person to take on the role of Milkweed's new guardian.

—

On a sunny afternoon in late June 2003, my last afternoon at Milkweed, I waited in my office until everyone else had left for the day. My briefcase was stuffed with the notes, photos, and messages I'd removed from the large corkboard behind my desk. The computer held more than a year's supply of titles to fill the pipeline while the next publisher was acquiring works for the future.

The desk drawers and the surface of my desk were, for the first time, empty, but the hefty bookcase across the office from my desk was completely filled with Milkweed Editions books. My thoughts were equally crowded, overflowing with recollections of meetings with writers in this and in former offices, as we discussed the manuscripts that would be transformed over time into the dynamic entities on those shelves—books. I was struck once again by my good fortune in having experienced so many eventful, demanding, fulfilling, indelible years in the company of readers and writers, time well spent.

On that summer afternoon when I left my office, I silently wished Milkweed Editions the very best—an enduring, aspirational, and meaningful future. On the occasion of Milkweed's fortieth anniversary, I can say with conviction that my wish has been fulfilled.

—EMILIE BUCHWALD

Here's an *amen* by John Caddy—
He writes: *Those plants that rely on wind to spread their seed are the pioneers that green disturbed ground, that prepare the soil for a second species group. Succession on scraped ground is Earth's green bandage.*

A milkweed pod
flowers its silks onto the wind.
The pebble-skin yawns, white
billows from the center,
a gust looses floss, the first flight
of seeds ride their silks
already high and free,

off to feed caterpillars
and turn them into kings—

What the wind is for.

THE MILKWEED
CHRONICLE PREFACES

WHERE DO WE COME FROM?
WHAT ARE WE?
WHERE ARE WE GOING?

Volume 1, Number 1, Winter 1980

"*D'où Venons Nous? Que Sommes Nous? Où Allons Nous?*"
—PAUL GAUGUIN

We invite you to join *Milkweed Chronicle* in an exploration of images, ideas, and themes expressed by poets and visual artists.

Milkweed Chronicle will offer a new source of public recognition for emerging talent in the arts of graphics and poetry and will serve as a focal point for collaborations between artistic disciplines. We also wish to call attention to ideas of artists of the past that have influenced the course of artistic investigation.

Milkweed Chronicle will publish poetry and visual explorations of every kind, including groups of drawings, prints, or photographs that communicate effectively independent of copy.

In this first issue, artists were invited to read the poems accepted for publication and to choose those poems or groupings of poems they wished to illustrate. In future issues, we intend to set up a dialogue between artists and poets. We would also like to receive collaborative projects. Artists and writers who wish to work together are invited to place an ad in our free classifieds; artists may wish to have their visuals displayed and their interests listed in VISIBLE, a display of images from an artist, with a brief statement of goals.

For our purposes, our large newspaper-size page is liberating, providing the space to publish the work of many poets and artists, enabling us to present the poems in an interesting framework, to allow for visual play under the control of professional visual editing, and to offer readers a publication that is through-designed in its juxtaposing of poems and visual art.

Guest artists will contribute to the design and layout of each issue; other artists will illustrate individual poems or groupings of poems. The concept of "through-design" does not mean that each poem will be—or should be!—illustrated. It does imply that care will be exercised to present each poem as advantageously as possible from the point of view of design.

The possibilities afforded by the double-page centerfold are intriguing. That space will be used for a large-scale graphic, either on its own or accompanied by a poem or poems or, as in this issue, by a guest column written by the artist. The centerfold is easily removed for poster-style display.

Our format allows the artist the freedom and visual excitement of a large performance space. We imagine that this opportunity will act as a stimulus to innovation and experiment that the size restrictions of most literary magazines do not permit. Given what is basically an ideal book format within a larger newspaper context, the widest range of possibilities is open for the exposition of visual poetics.

Eugene Delacroix commented that "most writing about art is by people who are not artists; thus, all the misconceptions." We agree. Because there are many excellent journals that feature book reviews and critical articles, we believe that our purposes are far better served by columns that are the personal commentaries of poets, visual artists, librettists, choreographers, dancers, musicians, directors—those who work directly in an individual or a collaborative art, or those who are concerned about the arts as teachers and students.

Each issue will present three or four guest columns. These brief essays may record the artist's thoughts about what it is like to work in the arts in this culture at this time, or attempt to verbalize the phenomenon of creating, or make a statement of principle, or deal with a point of technique.

Gemma Rossini Cullen's column in this issue is a description of her purpose and process in the creation of her arresting, intricate, and subtle series of pen-and-ink *Metamorphosis Drawings*.

Poet and teacher Phillip Dacey has stuck out his neck for a point of principle: in his brief, thorough, but unsententious essay, he uses a verbal scalpel to dissect the statements of those who believe that contemporary poets have no need for traditional poetic knowledge and training. Since the lines are sharply drawn on this issue, we hope to hear from you in a letter to the editor, perhaps in the form of a short essay of your own, if you subscribe to John Cage's notion that "rather than using your time to denounce what someone else has done, you should rather, if your feelings are critical, reply with a work of your own."

Greg Schaffner's column is a personal account of the problems and rewards inherent in the collaborative process. He raises questions that are of particular importance to us: namely, how can the visual artist and the poet find a way to work together that is mutually beneficial to them and to the work? How can they sustain the collaboration over a period of time? What elements must be present to transform the efforts of two individuals working with different methods in different art forms into a synergism that yields more than the sum of the two effects taken independently?

Perhaps the most persistent attempt by a practicing artist to understand and to describe what relationships are possible between different artistic disciplines was made by the painter Wassily Kandinsky, who wrote about the subject many times and over a period of many years. He and Franz Marc formed *Der Blaue Reiter* group (named after a 1903 canvas by Kandinsky) and exhibited not only their own work but also the work of Picasso, Arp, Braque, Klee, Nolde, and Derain. In 1912 they edited and published *Der Blaue Reiter*

Almanach, which called attention to folk art, primitive art, African and Asian art, medieval woodcuts and sculpture, and included articles on music by Schoenberg, Berg, and Webern. Of this extremely influential project, Kandinsky writes: "[Franz] Marc and I had thrown ourselves into painting but painting alone did not satisfy us. Then I had the idea of doing a 'synthesized' book which was to eliminate old narrow ideas and tear down the walls between the arts . . . and which was to demonstrate eventually that the question of art is not a question of form but one of artistic content."

Kandinsky believed that "the relationships in art are not necessarily ones of outward form, but are founded on an inner sympathy of meaning," that although each art is "something complete in itself," that the final goal of the arts, which is "knowledge and the refinement of the soul . . . obliterates external differences and reveals their inner identity."

We invite the artist's attempts to find "correspondences," to enlarge the possibilities of the individual art form, and we will be seeking those joint ventures that "are founded on an inner sympathy of meaning." When you come upon pages in this journal that do not rise to these expectations, judge us by the height of the attempt. There will be failures of technique and failures of illumination. Sometimes an aspiring failure sets off more significant reverberations than an easy success.

Milkweed Chronicle is a conference-field. We welcome the viewers and the visionaries, the supporters and the creators to these pages.

WALLS / WINDOWS

Volume 1, Number 2, Spring/Summer 1980

Our sense of limits and freedoms, for which walls and windows are but one set of props, is largely determined by the intellectual climate of the age into which we happen to be born.

The sixth-century monk Cosmas Indicopleustes, author of a widely distributed world geography, described the universe in biblical terms as a tabernacle, a box whose rounded lid was pierced by the jeweled windows we call stars, windows into the radiant eternity of the celestial realm. Though unreachable and unknowable, the stars were a link in the great chain of being that included men and beasts, vegetables and stones.

It was with the greatest reluctance that people gave up their notion of the stars as angels' peepholes, the many eyes through which their lives were seen, recorded, and judged; that concept was not materially altered for a thousand years.

The concept that the stars were actually gaseous aggregates, flaming in the vastness of the silences charted by Newton's math, was a source of loneliness and anxiety not only to Pascal but also to all of Western civilization. A sense of kinship with the universe was lost.

The strongbox of our century's expanding universe has been described by contemporary writers as firmly sealed. The graffiti they scrawl on the walls are various wordings of "no exit."

The poems of our times reflect this profound feeling of enclosure. They express a turning away from the universal, the general, anything that smacks of an earlier dogmatism. In 1905, G. K. Chesterton complained of a "total levity on the subject of cosmic philosophy."

Writers chose instead to concentrate on the world they could observe in detail at first hand. They looked more closely than ever before into the lighted windows of other lives, not as voyeurs but as intent geographers of the individual. Instead of turning a telescope on the sky, the writer focused a microscope on the psyche. Once the cosmos was secularized, the self became the source of mystery and new definitions of limits and freedoms for that exploration were formulated.

Two of this issue's essays examine the role of traditional forms in poetry in terms of the writer's conception of his freedoms and responsibilities. A number of the poems and graphics deal directly with concepts of limit, natural or imposed. "In Velvet" by Ann Chandonnet describes a world in which the welfare of an entire people appears to depend upon the minute observation of limits.

Another group of poems deals with that potent reminder of human limitation, death, the real or hidden subject of most serious poetry that is not love poetry, and of much of that as well. In the poetry of our time, one does not hear, "Death be not proud . . . Death, thou shalt die!" Dylan Thomas writes that death shall have no dominion, but it is difficult to imagine poems more dominated by death, or more death-haunted, than his. And although there are other poets who rage against the dying of the light, rage is not the most important emotion in contemporary poems about death and dying, except in the antiwar poems. A poem of controlled rage like Anthony Hecht's "More Light! More Light!"—surely one of the great poems of our age—does not cry out against the cruel necessity of dying but against the degradation of life by the living. Philip Levine's Spanish Civil War poems and Robert Bly's anti-Vietnam poems display this same Swiftian hatred for the depravity of our Yahoo species.

When contemporary poets talk of their own deaths, the mode is descriptive; the tone is contemplative; the emotions are varied, but acceptance is rarely absent; there is as much of a debt to the stoics and to Horace and to the Eastern contemplative tradition as to Sartre. The poems rise and fall and circle within nature. These poets face mortality without hope of heaven but without fear of hell, which, after all, the poems reveal, each of us carries with us in our private universe.

MOVEMENT / DANCE

Volume 1, Number 3, Fall 1980

The image of Shiva Nataraja, Lord of the Dance, surrounded by his aureole of fiery energy, dancing the fivefold dance of creation, preservation, destruction, veiling, and release, seems an appropriate one for our cover.

This issue celebrates energy, the energy expressed in the rhythm and movement of living forms and the energy of gigantic masses and subatomic particles notated by the statistics of quantum mechanics. The image of the universal dance is that of a complex harmony in which humans must find their part. Poets and artists of every culture have described the universal dance and have always been employed to devise and to depict the proper rituals of celebration.

This issue celebrates the rhythms that underlie our life-dances, the internal rhythms that keep our hearts pounding and air in our lungs, and the pulse of each day, each season.

This season celebrates the idea of spontaneity, of play, the counterpoint to the fixed and inevitable clocking-rhythms; it celebrates our ability to abandon ourselves to the unexpected, to release ourselves to joy.

LIVING IN SPACE-TIME

Volume 2, Number 1, Winter 1981

Where do we live? Confined, most of us, most of the time, in the universe that Newton built; a universe that is a triumph of law and order, of three dimensions in space and one dimension in time that thrusts us always forward toward the moment when we fall out of matter and disappear.

Must we live within these boundaries? Quantum physicists suggest to us that we need not, that we are capable of an expansion of habitat that depends upon our perspective of consciousness.

Poets and artists make constant use of the mind's ability to imagine itself elsewhere, to stop the clock of the outside world while another portion of reality unfolds before us.

This alteration of "real" time occurs in the work of both poets of essence and poets of existence.

"Here," says the poet of essence, holding out a few glowing grains on his palm, "I make you a present of what I have refined out of time. All the rest is mere pitchblende."

"Here," says the poet of existence, extending a slice of the life-hologram, "I have gathered reality in this construct; all dimensions are presented as faithfully as the laser of my imagination can focus them."

When we accept either vision, we escape from the apparent rigidity of the universe in the company of a poem, a work of art, and an act of music. Alvaro Cardona-Hine's essay in this issue, "The Time of the Poet," describes the task of the poet as that ability to lift us out of the illusion of time.

What attributes of mind allow us to exist in the possible elsewhere as well as in the immediate here? In *The Biological Basis of Imagination*, R. W. Gerard describes the exquisite complexity of the network of the several billion nerve cells that make up our brain, each of which is participating in dynamic electrochemical and electromagnetic reactions:

> *Messages bombard the nerve cells along these many paths, some pushing it to action and some to quietude . . . Further, the nerve cell is being influenced by the blood passing it, the oxygen and sugar it receives, the salts that bathe it, the electric currents from its neighbors, the temperature at which it finds itself, by drugs which reach it . . .*

The question that arises for discussion: is this aggregate of nerve cells, the brain, a closed-system computer rearranging the sensory stimuli it receives, or is it a receiver whose function is filtering out unnecessary information from the cosmic bombardment of the universe?

Sir John Eccles suggests in *The Neurophysiological Basis of Mind* the concept that the brain functions as an information filter, allowing in only as much data as we need to construct reality and to focus on a particular aspect of it. Aldous Huxley refers to the same idea in *The Doors of Perception*, namely that the function of the brain is *eliminative*, that it protects us from being swamped by the deluge of universal information, that each one of us is potentially "Mind at Large."

Huxley's participation in a monitored mescalin experiment enabled him to experience what takes place when the filtering mechanism is tampered with:

> *Place and time cease to be of much interest . . . Not, of course, that the category of space had been abolished . . . Space was still*

there; but it had lost its predominance. The mind was primarily concerned, not with measures and locations, but with being and meaning. And along with the indifference to space there went an even completer indifference to time.

"There seems to be plenty of it" was all I would answer when the investigator asked me to say what I felt about time.

"Plenty of it," but exactly how much was irrelevant. I could, of course, have looked at my watch; but my watch, I knew, was in another universe. My actual experience had been, was still, of an indefinite duration or alternatively of a perpetual present made up of one continually changing apocalypse.

The picture that Huxley gives us is strikingly in accord with what Einstein's special theory of relativity tells us is the most useful way to think of the space-time continuum—as a nonmoving picture in which events *are*—that instead of imagining events unfolding with the passage of time, we should imagine that everything that was, is, or will be is already there in the structure of space-time.

Space and time in the Minkowski-Einstein block universe are connected at every point in a universal web (much like the description that Gerard gives us of the network of nerve cells); one coordinate cannot be changed without changing another. Further, the gravity of mass produces a curvature in space-time, so that time flows at different rates according to the distribution of mass. A clock advanced closer to the density of a black hole's gravity runs more and more slowly. There is no single time that permeates the universe, no absolute time.

Like the people in Plato's parable of the cave, we are chained to our mind-structure of the world; we see only the shadows cast by the firelight. It is difficult to escape out into the sun. When we return to the cave and its puny flickering, describing the quality of the light outside, who inside the cave will believe that we are not mad?

The quantum physicists have been advancing out of the cave for better than seventy-five years, but for the most part they have couched their news of "out there" in mathematical formulae. Only recently has the good news been told in language that sounds startlingly similar to what we are accustomed to hearing from consciousness research writers and to reading in ancient belief systems:

> *Why are all things neither departing nor coming? Because*
> *though they are characterized with the masks of individuality*
> *and generality, these masks coming and departing neither come*
> *nor depart . . . Why are all things permanent? Because though*
> *they take forms . . . they take really no such forms and in reality,*
> *there is nothing born, nothing passing away.*
>
> LANKAVATARA SUTRA

The quantum physicists state that one cannot observe something without changing it—that the physical universe does not exist independent of the thoughts of the participator. As the physicist J. A. Wheeler puts it, "The vital act is the act of participation. 'Participator' is the incontrovertible new concept given by quantum mechanics. It strikes down the term 'observer' of classical theory, the man who stands safely behind the thick glass wall and watches what goes on without taking part. It can't be done, quantum mechanics says."

Jack Sarfetti, a physicist whose special interest is the nature of consciousness, writes: "The idea that consciousness is at the root of the material universe can be traced back to Parmenides, Bishop Berkeley, Alfred North Whitehead, and astronomer James Jeans, who said that the universe looks less and less like a big machine and more and more like a great thought. In physics, the point of view was initiated, perhaps unwittingly, by Niels Bohr and Werner Heisenberg (whose work on the uncertainty principle shows that the influence of the observer is unavoidable) and is now being carried forward by a number of other visionary physicists." Physicists and biologists are producing experiments to demonstrate that consciousness at its most fundamental level is a quantum process, that the leaps of mind all of us make, and that artists especially desire to make, are a manifestation of a universal connectedness.

In the moments when the filter control of the brain blinks off, the stuff of the universe pours in, and we are mind moving upon silence, like Yeats's long-legged fly upon the stream. We are aware of the I and the not-I simultaneously. As Jorge Luis Borges describes in "A New Refutation of Time":

> *Time is a river which sweeps me along, but I am the river; it is a tiger which mangles me, but I am the tiger; it is a fire which consumes me, but I am the fire. The world, unfortunately, is real; I, unfortunately, am Borges.*

TRANSLATIONS /
CONVERSIONS / EQUIVALENTS

Volume 2, Number 2, Spring/Summer 1981

The literary translator has endless ways to go wrong, numberless blind alleys of maze down which to stumble.

Each culture is its own maze, its own assemblage of gestures, visual signals, language, filled with meaning and reference special to itself. The flavor of a culture is distinctive enough so that we actually have certain qualities in mind when we speak of it; when we name a culture, we conjure certain image and idea clusters that the name evokes.

A translator of literature must have the ability to make a transference of all this into another tongue, to convert what is already precisely imagined in one form into an equivalent work that represents the original well and truly in meaning and spirit.

A translator of literature must slide inside the body and mind of a culture, must see through its eyes and imagine with its conceptions. There are various methods of perceiving the world: to think / to feel / to see / to understand / to will / to judge / to dream—these represent only some of them, and of course they are mingled in different proportions in each society and presented uniquely in the bone structure of a language's grammar—its sounds, forms, and syntax— and in its robes of tone and nuance of expression.

A translator of literature also has to believe in a larger human sphere, has to believe in the necessity of crossing boundaries to make contacts, to reconcile the misunderstandings that language separateness can create. Paradoxically, it appears that at this time when the possibilities of communication are greater than they have ever been, the spirit of the age shrinks back to nationalism, regionalism, and tribalism, and to an impatience with what is different or unknown; few of us dare to ask—what does the universe desire from me? Or even to imagine that there might be such a question.

This issue features the work of twelve translators of contemporary poetry. Each translator provides a few words of comment about the poet she/he has chosen; words that demonstrate the bond of affectionate respect and regard between translators themselves. Edmund Keeley's essay, "Thoughts on Literary Translation," vividly traces the history of the art in this country over the past thirty years; he is cautiously optimistic.

MUSIC / RHYTHM

Volume 2, Number 3, Fall 1981

The visual presentation of several different texts occupying more or less the same space creates something of the texture of everyday life, in which the ear is bombarded by a jumble of noises, some of which decode into signals that have meaning to us.

We bring to the external world an ability to assimilate sounds, to concentrate on a few and to screen out others, but we are ourselves a universe of counterpointing internal rhythms. We are not silent within. Our bones oscillate, tuned to the other vibrations within the body envelope. We feel either attuned or in discord with the envelope of sound moving around us. "We have no earlids," R. Murray Schafer reminds us in *The Tuning of the World* (Alfred A. Knopf, 1977). We are at the mercy of our environment.

The varied sounds and rhythms of the natural world have been reproduced in our writing and in our music since human beings began to write and compose. But for most of us, the sound environment is not one of birdsong and rustling grass. The sounds and pulses of the machine form our sonic web. We protect ourselves by dropping these noises into a mental limbo, heard but not attended to. John Cage suggested, as long ago as 1937, that we use noise—listen to it, record it, integrate it—as a musical component—and make our own noise.

In the past sixty years, poets have experimented vigorously with sound poetry—utilizing speech rhythms, jazz counterpointing of beats, and the revival of a chanting style that owes allegiance to bardic traditions, a human delight in hearing and feeling sounds as they resonate in the breath cavities. Many of the poems in this issue of *Milkweed Chronicle* would not be as effective read to an audience as they are on the page. There is no value judgment involved—it is simply true that the greater the complexity of thought, the higher the density of images, the more subtle the word rhythms, the less likely it is that a poem will be enjoyed when it is read aloud.

The poet writing for a listening audience must learn how much a listener can absorb in a given time frame. The poet who writes to be heard is functioning as an a cappella musician, a new bard who uses the breath and word equivalents of the skilled percussionist. In the era of industrial drone and the noise wall of musak and the transistor, we have a craving to hear the varying pulsations of human life.

WAKING, SLEEPING, DREAMING

Volume 3, Number 1, Winter 1982

As we prepared for this issue, we were fortunate in having access to the resources of an extraordinary exhibit, *Artifacts: An Exhibition of Dreamwork*, sponsored by the Minnesota Archetypal Study Center (MASC), featuring contributions of more than fifty exhibitors.

More submissions arrived for the "The Sleepers and the Awakening" from writers around the country than for any previously announced theme. Envelopes of various sizes and bulk were wedged tightly together in our post office box every time we checked it, and the poems in the envelopes were almost all poems about sleeping and dreaming.

We were surprised at how few of the poems we received concerned themselves with awakening, literal or symbolic. The subject is obviously not popular.

The notion of waking up has a hard edge to it, something of gritting the teeth, something of the way one feels at three o'clock in the morning on a cross-country bus trip with two more days to go.

Difficult questions occur when one chooses to be awake. Awake to what? Paying attention to what? Deciding: at what level of illusion am I content to live? To face the genuine nature of life on this planet is to court terror. We have a good instinctive sense of this terror early in our lives, and if we are to live in this world without weeping daily, some part of us slumbers.

Being awake and staying awake, particularly at this moment in a society that's looking around to find its spirit, is tough. Like digging a path through snow from the house to the sidewalk—for the fifth day in a row. That's the here and now, the inescapable. Carol Bly's essay, "The Gifts of Psychology: Not Dreams But Living with General Merv Blastad," tackles the idea that though it's easier to look away from the ugliness of suffering, to fall into a death-sleep of pain avoidance, it's within the capability of each of us to effect change, if we are willing to risk being rebuffed and disdained.

It's especially easy now, with so much winter around us, to fall inward, to stay within daydream as much as possible. Our boots, not our feet, touch the frozen sidewalk; we're isolated from one another and from the outside world in our layers of winter swaddling.

Perhaps we need the daydreams more at this season—and there's no question that we need daydreams and night dreams if we're going to have the physical and emotional energy to be awake. When the forms of the outside world are muffled and the colors are brighter within, it makes sense to do some protective daydreaming, to float inward toward a live center of self and reaffirm its presence.

And, if we valued night sleeping for no other reason, we would treasure it as the buffer between the efforts and weariness of the day that's past and the attempts to feel, to imagine, and to accomplish in the day to come. A night's sleep enables us to say to ourselves in the morning, "Okay, dummy; try again."

Although scientists have various theories about why sleep is beneficial, there appears to be general agreement that a benefit takes place from both quiet sleep (non-REM sleep) and dreaming sleep (REM sleep). In a process that takes more than an hour, we sleep our way down though well-measured levels of sleep to level 4, the most profound level of unconsciousness that we experience short of death; in this state, an electroencephalogram records the brain waves in slow, jagged patterns. Then we begin the ascent to REM sleep. Dream sleep is triggered in the pons of the hindbrain, a late mammalian evolutionary development; presumably, therefore, dreaming sleep is a useful mammalian adaptation.

During REM sleep, brain temperature and blood flow increase, as do the pulse and breathing rates, and the eyes dart back and forth under closed lids. Scientists who study REM sleep postulate that many of the phenomena we experience in our dreams, such as sensations of falling or flying, are the results of the thinking brain's attempt to make sense of confusing signals; cells in the brainstem involved in movement or perception are sending messages to the brain while at the same time the muscles controlling movement are inhibited. Drs. J. Allan Hobson and Robert McCarley speculate that "dreams may be . . . a kind of brain tune-up crucial to preparing the organism for behavioral competence" (Dianne Hales, *The Complete Book of Sleep*, Addison-Wesley Publishing Company, 1981). Or, for that matter, dreams may be the brain's way of assimilating the intellectual and emotional input of the previous day.

This kind of research need not be viewed as science's cold water dashed on the serious study of dream interpretation; on the contrary, the neuroscientist's investigation of the way in which brain processes function discloses more and more the integration of mind and body. "The dream," Jung writes, "is a little hidden door in the innermost and most secret parts of the psyche."

The fact that we know more about the biochemical circuitry that operates the door doesn't make the stuff of dreams less intriguing or an understanding of their significance to us less important and revealing. The scientist's ability to differentiate various sleep levels is a confirmation of the centuries old Indian Mandukya Upanishad's analysis of three of the four elements of the mystic syllable *aum* into waking consciousness, dream consciousness, and deep, dreamless sleep. The more we learn of the intricacies of our neuro-chemical-electrical selves, the more obvious it becomes that our physical makeup predisposes us both to reverie and to action, to the use of symbols as well as tools, and to a delight in myth that not even exposure to a daily paper and television can expunge.

Three *Milkweed Chronicle* covers: "Shaking the Bones," cover art by Arne Nyen; "Magic," cover art by Barbra Nei; "Limits," cover art by R.W. Scholes

A reading celebrating Open Book; Emilie Buchwald, Bill Holm, Jim Moore, Faith Sullivan

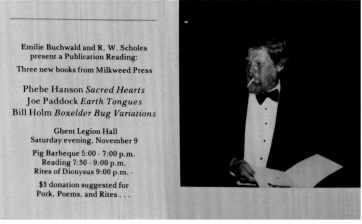

Bill Holm at the Milkweed reading for *Boxelder Bug Variations*, *Sacred Hearts*, and *Earth Tongues* in Ghent, Minnesota, 1986

Carol Bly, author of *Backbone*; *The Passionate, Accurate Story*; *Changing the Bully Who Rules the World*; and *My Lord Bag of Rice: New and Selected Stories*

Steven Sorman and Patricia Hampl, creators of *Spillville*, in 1987

Milkweed staff, 1988. Top row: Deborah Keenan, Marilyn Matthews, Mark Schultz, Steve Chase. Bottom row, R. W. Scholes, Emilie Buchwald

An invitation to Milkweed's Tenth Birthday Party. Please note: the first letter of Judith Guest's and Joe Paddock's name is missing.

Eighteen authors reading from their work at Milkweed Editions's Tenth Birthday Party. Top row: Bill Meissner, Phebe Hanson, John Caddy, Bill Holm, Margaret Hasse. Second row: Carol Bly, Joe Paddock, Diane Glancy, David Mura, Judith Guest, Jim Stowell. Bottom row: Philip Dacey, Deborah Keenan, Jim Moore, Jill Breckenridge, Patricia Weaver Francisco, Tim Francisco

John Caddy, author of *Eating the Sting*, *The Color of Mesabi Bones*, and *Morning Earth*

Larry Watson, author of *Montana 1948* and *Justice*

Bapsi Sidhwa, author of *Cracking India*, *The Crow Eaters*, and *An American Brat*

American Booksellers Association Convention, 1995. Beth Olson, Milkweed's managing editor, and Bob Breck, Milkweed's marketing and sales director

American Booksellers Association Convention, 1995. Annick Smith, author of *Homestead*; Larry Watson, author of *Justice*; David Haynes, author of *Somebody Else's Mama*

Faith Sullivan, author of *The Empress of One* and *What a Woman Must Do*

David Haynes, author of *Somebody Else's Mama*, *Live at 5*, *All American Dream Dolls*, and the children's titles *The Gumma Wars* and *West 7th Street Wildcats*

Paul Gruchow, author of *Grass Roots*, *Boundary Waters*, and *The Necessity of Empty Places*

Ken Kalfus, author of *Thirst* and *Pu-239 and Other Russian Fantasies*

Robert Redford's special reading at Sundance for *Testimony*, 1996. Authors: Bill Kittredge, Ann Zwinger, Richard Shelton, Don Snow, Rick Bass, Ellen Meloy, Stephen Trimble. Milkweed invitees: Gayle Peterson, Milkweed's executive director (kneeling, second from left, second row), Susan Borneman, Milkweed's board chair (fourth from left, second row), and Emilie Buchwald, publisher (middle, second row from the top)

Janisse Ray, author of *Ecology of a Cracker Childhood* and *Wild Card Quilt*

Scott Slovic, founder of the Association for the Study of Literature and the Environment (ASLE)

Pattiann Rogers, author of *Firekeeper: New and Selected Poems, Eating Bread and Honey,* and *Song of the World Becoming: New and Collected Poems*

Seth Kantner, author of *Ordinary Wolves*

Milkweed staff in their new offices at Open Book, 2000.
Top row: Sid Farrar, Molly Bromert, Greg Larson, Laurie Buss, Erik Norsted. Bottom row: Hilary Reeves, Emilie Buchwald, Susan Doerr, Anja Welsh, Elizabeth Cooper

CEREMONY / RITUAL:
SUMMONING THE LIVE

Volume 3, Number 2, Spring/Summer 1982

To summon, if need be, the souls of the dead has been one of the functions of ritual, as it has been to pray to the dead for favor, to propitiate the dead by our actions, to gain insights from the dead in our psychic wanderings. Warriors eat liver, heart, and brain of a slain enemy to gain his power. Congregants eat the body and drink of the blood of the willing sacrifice to partake of and share in its essence.

Cultures that have rigidly ritualized every one of life's activities bind the individual in a web of great tension. In such cultures, nonperformance of the rites is a cause for serious alarm; the level of frustration and the possibility of making an error are high. In such a culture there is significant danger of the individual's energies being totally consumed by ritual obligations, and of the occasional individual who runs amok, seizing the ceremonial sword and using it on someone unfortunate enough to be nearby. Ritual continues to be felt as a live weight.

In contemporary societies, ritual is often felt to be empty, a sham performance, or prescribed words and actions from which real meaning has fled. We feel a sense of loss, a sinking instead of an ecstatic rising, particularly at times of holiday, when the ceremony of celebration gives us not the real but an empty form.

We're slow to recognize that when the need for a particular rite disappears, the rite persists only as discarded skin that the living creature shed—and moved on from.

That live essence we seek must be allowed to find its own new form. Writers who attempt to summon the live must balance, as a shaman is required to balance, on the threshold between worlds, walking the narrow, tricky path between the interior world of self and the outside world, to offer something of themselves as sacrifice in order to do the cliff-leaping, the ledge-walking, in order to attain some vision with which they and we can return to daily life.

Phebe Hanson's essay, "Here I Am," describes a living ritual that grows with each day's images—journal keeping. Michael Kincaid's constructed essay is an unusual attempt to heighten and invoke, to know feelingly by using form as well as content to create "The Ritual of Being." Edith Bruck's poems give us the taste of the hard, dry, dark bread of brutalized existence. David Ignatow and Ruth Roston insist that poems should live and dance and make love. Simon Vinkenoog tells us that existence calls out to us for participation, for action. We must listen well to know that when we write we are required, in William Stafford's words, "to give back a voice, / be a temple in a temple," to hold a ceremony within ourselves to summon the live.

THE WORLD AS THEATER

Volume 3, Number 3, Fall 1982

This issue presents cuttings from three contemporary plays with the hope that you'll want to experience more of these works. Marisha Chamberlain's note to the reader regarding her excerpt from *Winter Camera* contains important advice for your reading of each cutting: imagine, in addition to hearing the dialogue, that you are able to see the action and reaction taking place between the characters, the glances they exchange, the gesture of a hand, the piece of stage business that illuminates the meaning of a conversation.

The excerpts from Martha Boesing's *Ashes, Ashes, We All Fall Down* give only a sketch of the plot; the focus is on the scenes that describe in clinical detail the effects of the detonation of a nuclear bomb. These scenes exemplify Bertolt Brecht's concept of theater as an instrument of assessment. Brecht wanted the audience at his plays to leave the theater *thinking*, not succumbing to emotional ennui; angry, not despairing; determined to take action.

The inclusion of a scene from Ted Tally's *Terra Nova* was prompted by Lou Salerni's thoughts about the play in his essay, "Director As Lover." *Terra Nova* is a play rich in evocative language and strong characterization. Above all, *Terra Nova* is an examination of cultural values. Scott's antagonist, Roald Amundsen, the leader of the rival Norwegian expedition, is brought into the play as a commentator and observer, a character only Scott sees and talks with.

Their scenes together force consideration of the play's basic questions: What is decent behavior in an alien, hostile world? What is the price of reputation? At what price does one buy survival?

In "How to Write a Play," George Bernard Shaw comments: "All interpreters of life in action, noble or ignoble, find their instrument in theatre." Of all the arts, theater has always had the greatest opportunity to show us to ourselves—and thus to comment on human behavior.

And why? Because watching live theater is an act of participation. Theater draws its strength from the response of the audience to the action on stage. The audience is a vital element in the chemistry of a live performance. The audience takes part in an exchange with the performers—an exchange of energy. An audience will forgive much that is amateurish in a production if its members experience seriousness of intent and commitment of effort. In a sense, the term "theatre of involvement" is a redundancy.

Unfortunately, the same sense of involvement does not occur in the presentation of world news by the media. Television flashes scenes of carnage before our eyes, allowing us no time to feel the meaning of what we see. The news is presented as divertissement; subtly, it is packaged as entertainment of a kind. We are made easy-chair spectators of war, terrorism, massacre, and mass starvation, sights that seem at once normal and remote. The world is brought to us in the form of film clips and news releases, a theater of desperate and brutal acts.

The passivity we experience, the lack of response, is, in part, a lack of ability to feel that which does not immediately touch us. That lack points out the importance of the presence of models in the culture that are life-affirming. John Gardner's essay "On Moral Fiction" addresses the question in these words: "Real art creates myths a society can live with instead of die by, and clearly our society is in need of such myths." Art of this order "holds up models of decent behavior; characters whose basic goodness and struggle against confusion, error, and evil in themselves and others gives firm intellectual and emotional support to our own struggle. Nor should these models be stereotypic or sentimental—but rather individual, the result of a total creative process which involves a rigorous mode of thought, a detailing of the concrete, an individuality which does not depend on realism." The art we can live with rather than die by is an art that places value on making conscious choices, an art that reminds us that our choices have consequences—that recognizes each of us as a participant.

GEOGRAPHIES / GEOLOGIES

Volume 4, Number 1, Winter 1983

Men and women living in the northern middle ages would have had little understanding of or sympathy for Wordsworth's nature poetry. You long for wild nature only once you are no longer afraid of starving in the pitiless forest, or of being clubbed by one of nature's noblemen. Forests and mountains defied man's civilizing hand. Fear of demonic spirits lurking there prevented casual enjoyment of nature in the northern countries of that era.

It was only in a fairly recent time—the eighteenth century—that northerners looked at mountains as sublime, majestic, and beautiful rather than as foul blemishes on earth's smooth face created by the Flood, just punishment for man's early wickedness.

Our present concern with preserving wilderness and our sense of renewal and refreshment in its uncivilized grandeur are fairly new ideas in the history of man on the planet.

The Greeks and the Romans had a kindlier view of nature: they peopled it with nature spirits of varied character not necessarily hostile to human beings. And they wrote of a vanished Golden Age, an ideal accommodation between man and nature, whose only law was harmonious coexistence.

In this age of lead, we look out upon our world: oil-slicked oceans, strip-mined mountains, eroded croplands, blighted cities whose snarled highways lead to dormitories and shopping centers.

It's painful to see the magnitude of the mess. Because we know, like it or not, that we are creatures of place, and that this world is our place.

We feel that connection instinctively in grade school, running the tips of our fingers over the mountains and plains of the physical relief globe. We're imprinted with the geography of the place in which we grow up; we can touch it, see it, walk it again in memory. And we count, deeply, on the security of our own microenvironment, a home base, a safe haven, the personal landscape we make around us.

Many of the poems in this issue are filled with the beauty of a piece of earth, the exaltation of living in place, of becoming part of a landscape, feeling its pulse and moving to its tempos. The particularity, the idiosyncrasies of place are revealed as the features of a loved individual face, and there is gratitude in these poems for being allowed to live with, rather than against, the land. To dwell in harmony with one place on earth is to experience the holiness of a Golden Age, to live in communion with rather than as a parasite.

A recent science magazine article shows a photo enlargement of skin mites the size of elephants bearing down upon a flake of loose skin. We are equally creatures of our host, the earth, scrounging upon and beneath its skin, dependent upon it for existence and sustenance. And if our truly genial and giving host dies by our rapacious parasitizing—there is no other-where for humans to go, no other home. Ron Kroese's article about the Land Stewardship Project and the poems of Joe and Nancy Paddock address urgent facts.

RIDDLES / PUZZLES / MAZES / GAMES

Volume 4, Number 2, Spring/Summer 1983

When Euripides says, "Count no man happy until he's dead," he refers to the notion that we are players in a life-game whose outcome is uncertain until the final moment. We may achieve contentment, honor, riches, and wisdom, and still, all can be taken away; the idea that we are counters in a god-game has fascinated writers in every culture. God and the devil contend for man's soul not only in Marlowe's *Doctor Faustus* and in Goethe's *Faust*, but in the literature of many countries.

Human beings are gamesters to the core; we don't simply write of life as the ultimate game, we invent societies with arbitrary rules, including role-playing and rigidly defined moves for the players. To "play the game" is to learn to obey, without much thought, the dictates of one's culture, if one wants to be rewarded—pass GO and collect $200, or reach the eighth square and assume a power position.

In every culture, however, there are those who question the rationale of its particular game. That posture of stepping back— of observing one's society and the assumptions on which it's built— is taken on by the artist, not necessarily by choice but by the nature of art as exploration, as a walking beyond the known perimeters.

The artist moves outside the culture to look at its framework. We can recognize that we are part of a particular game only when we are given a vista from which to view it. In Lewis Carroll's *Through the Looking-Glass*, Alice has some idea of what she is about to encounter when she stands with the Red Queen on a hill overlooking the countryside and sees that it is divided into squares—a chessboard world. At that moment she has perspective.

And perspective really seems to make a difference. Your frame of reference is the window that encloses your intellectual vista. Keith Gunderson's series of poems, "The Authoritative Window," is an elegant and witty exploration of Schopenhauer's concept of the world as Will and Representation—how we mix ourselves into what we see.

Riddling, puzzling, and maze-making are coding processes. We take information and deliberately scramble it or disguise it for the shock of pleasure in the decoding and reassembling, or to conceal it from the enemy or the uninitiated. After wandering in mental darkness, the "answer" strikes us like a floodlight of revelation.

Writers, of course, are endlessly intrigued by the fact that words have the potential of being both precise and ambiguous—that a line of poetry can carry several different cargoes to the reader at the same time. Poets rely on the ability of language to name and to veil simultaneously as a way of giving the reader the rich sense of delight and insight that the answer to a good riddle gives. But in a poem, the mystery doesn't evaporate with an "answer." William Meissner's poem, "The Game," for example, a highly structured word game, gives the metaphor of the life-as-game in striking images, allowing the reader to participate directly and emotionally without making the game itself any the less mysterious.

A number of poems in this issue adhere to the "rules of the game" without losing the fresh and the vivid qualities that mark a work of art. The renga by Young, Sato, and Little is one excellent case in point; the form is defined by the exuberance, and sensitivity is deep.

One derivation of the word *game* is "to leap, or gambol joyfully." This issue celebrates the human impulse to "leap joyfully." We invite you to play.

New Games in the Culture

The new video games gobble the time of the user, and so far, the games are primitive—eat the monsters before they eat you or stay out of range of the space invaders who are trying to vaporize you. But the video game controls require skill; they may be the fore-runner of the space flight console of the future; the screen itself could become, for example, the projection arena for an embryo form of poetry that requires the player to make word responses to bursts of colored light, or to respond, image for image, to a poet's input; after all, there are programmable machines that have the po-tential to become sophisticated learning tools or a new art form that's a synthesis of word, light, and sound. Perhaps instead of ig-noring or worrying about a computerized future, writers and artists should consider shaping it. The future of more than these games will depend on who does the programming and how deeply the artistic imagination is employed. The rule for any computer pro-gram is garbage in, garbage out.

Adventure games such as Dungeons and Dragons have also exploded in popularity. These games are an exciting departure from the board game that transforms your fellow player into an opponent, the games of strategy that teach you to outwit, outbuy, or outgeneral your fellow player.

M.A.R. Barker, a professor of East Asian languages, has in-vented a popular boardless game called Tékumel: Empire of the Petal Throne. The game involves fantasy role-playing and is, in ef-fect, Barker says, a participatory novel-adventure generated and continued by the referee and the players. The players work as com-panions rather than opponents; they must role-play, and think of their characters as real-life citizens of the particular realm they in-habit. They must think about geography, sociology, religion. They must understand character interaction and be able to imagine them-selves vicariously in new situations. And they must expect their ac-tions to have consequences. The give-and-take of the story-making process is not unlike the collaborative writing that goes on in experimental theater groups. Although luck and a good roll of the dice are helpful, the message of these games, generally, is that rewards come from exercising the imagination, using good judgment, and working with others. Not bad.

THE SHAPES OF LIGHT

Volume 4, Number 3, Fall 1983

Our sight is confined in that portion of the electromagnetic spectrum of wavelengths between 3,900 to 7,700 angstroms. A pitifully small range. Out of our inadequacy have come the instruments of light that open the world to us—allow us to see farther, closer, deeper, and to break light into its component colors.

Artists are working with new tools to achieve old aims. The future may give us poets of the holograph and artists who work with the structures revealed by micrographs. We may be able to contemplate environmental sculptures created with the light of fiber optics and cities illuminated by diffraction towers in the brilliant colors of visible light.

The challenge for artists, however, will remain the same—to take the materials of the age and provide new perspectives, to allow us to look at the world as if seeing it for the first time, and to create out of an individual vision that which gives light to other human beings.

THE POET DREAMING IN THE
ARTIST'S HOUSE

Volume 5, Number 1, Winter 1984

Seeing the world is our principal means of entering into it.

The eye takes in line and shape, caresses contour, and is stimulated by the play of light and color. A work of art is seen at once,
whole and entire. Although poets have the possibility of suspending
a reader in time, they have envied artists this direct and immediate
access to sensation and emotion, while they must communicate in-
directly through the symbols of written language—hieroglyphs that
exclude those who cannot interpret them. "The author is obliged to
address himself to the mind before he can address the heart," Paul
Gauguin wrote in 1888. Poets, however, have been fascinated by the
challenge of making word pictures of works of art for the minds and
hearts of readers.

A sketch of the relationship between poetry and the visual arts
from classical antiquity to the present, such as Phyllis Janik presents
in her annotated bibliography, demonstrates a long and vigorous tradition of this literary pictorialism.

Toward the end of the nineteenth century, when both artists
and poets had sophisticated their technical abilities to create mirror images of the physical world, artists like Gauguin and the poet

Stéphane Mallarmé no longer considered that ability as a worthy aim of art or poetry. Instead, they believed that only the imagination and the expression of the individual were the proper province of art and poetry. Charles Baudelaire's belief that "the whole of the visible universe is only a storehouse of images and signs . . . that the imagination must digest and transform" was shared by poets such as Paul Verlaine, J.-K. Huysmans, and Stéphane Mallarmé, and artists like Gauguin, Odilon Redon, Maurice Denis, and Edvard Munch.

In 1914, Franz Marc writes that "the contemplation of the world has become the penetration of the world." Wassily Kandinsky, his friend and associate in *Der Blaue Reiter Almanach*, reiterates the idea that the subject matter and focus of art is "in the mystic content. Everything has a secret soul, which is silent more often than it speaks." "To give voice to the secret soul of things, to the ghostly aspect of things that only rare individuals see," as Marc Chagall puts it, is the artist's quest. The artist's journey must take him to the innermost sources of creation, Paul Klee believed, "as far as may be toward that secret ground where primal law feeds growth" to "render the secretly perceived . . . visible."

These ideas are restated by Howard Nemerov in his poem "The Painter Dreaming in the Scholar's House," from which we take our title. A meditation of singular nobility and beauty, written in memory of the painters Paul Klee and Paul Terrace Feeley, this poem might stand as a credo for the ideas of many twentieth-century artists who "sing the secret history of the mind." The first verse stanza echoes Klee's words: "The painter's eye follows relation out. / His work is not to paint the visible. / He says, it is to render visible." The vision of wholeness in the artist's mind is the dream, the "emblem to us in this life of thought."

The poets write about both historical and contemporary art with the resources and prejudices of the late twentieth century. "Nobody paints as he likes," writes the French artist Jean Bezaine. "All a painter can do is to will with all his might the painting his age is capable of," a statement as true for poets as for painters. Modern physics has shown that the role played by an observer becomes *part* of the experiment. As one physicist puts it, "The vital act is the act of participation. 'Participator' is the incontrovertible new concept given by quantum mechanics." Studies of the psyche have come to much the same conclusions; we interact with what we encounter. We make a difference in what we see. These poets are participators rather than examiners or dissociated observers. They choose to walk into the artist's house of vision and visions seeking language fresh enough and transparent enough to communicate their responses. They use the artist's techniques of collage, of commenting upon a found object, of utilizing accident in composition.

Picasso's comment that "the artist is a receptacle for emotions that come from all over the place; from the sky, from the earth, from a scrap of paper, from a passing shape, from a spider's web" is equally relevant for the contemporary poet who projects his spirit into the mysterious and "secret soul" of which Klee writes.

When we read and discussed these poems, they seemed to fall readily into four groupings. "Portraits of the Artist" are reflections on individual artists, and on the character of the artist's achievement. "Scenes" are word pictures of specific settings within paintings. "Still Lives" distill impressions of the subjects and objects depicted in works of art. "The Thing Itself" contains poems that concern the nature of art—its function in an individual's daily life, its relation to external nature, and its necessity as an outpouring of the human spirit.

These poems affirm for us the fact that the impulse to make art and to write poems rises out of the same desire to sing "the secret history of the mind," to extend the boundaries of the imagination and to give us what our lives would be barren without. We invite you to walk through the gallery they represent and to experience their depth, their humor and color, as participants in these visions, not unmoved.

GENDER

Volume 5, Number 2, Spring/Summer 1984

Sex change is quite normal in a number of fish species, especially among tropical fish. Sex changers are found in at least twenty-three families in seven separate orders of fish. Within a few hours after the death of the sole male in a group of cleaner wrasses, the largest female begins to exhibit male behavior; in a few weeks, her ovaries will have completely shifted to sperm production. Gorgeous red-and-gray plaid female stoplight parrotfish turn into rainbowed-blue male stoplight parrotfish when they become older and, therefore, larger.

A fish called the indigo hamlet (indecisive habits?) changes sex several times a day. During the courtship rites, a pair will determine which will assume the passive male role and which the active female role. After spawning, they switch and spawn again, with as many as five alternations in a single mating.

If the indigo hamlet had the ability to speak and to write, we would be spared the writing of manifestos on the rights and privileges of one particular sex vis-à-vis the other. Rather, we might have a lucid commentary on the experience of each and on the experiences common to both.

As vertebrate mammals who live on land, carry our young internally, and bear only a few offspring, our reproductive anatomy is too fixed and too complex for an easy exchange of sexes. We cannot know firsthand, as a Nassau grouper or a Mexican hogfish can, the perspective of a female and then that of a male. By their sex shift, these fish have maximized the reproductive possibilities open to them at each stage of their lives.

Human beings come into the world without any gender choice. Soon enough—in early infancy, many trained observers believe— we take on the gender roles of our society, the attitudes, behaviors, and motivations culturally associated with each sex. These roles will affect our play, our education, and our life's work. We become trapped in the "Gender Maze" that Toni A. H. McNaron writes of so eloquently. We look across what seems a Grand Canyon at those individuals who were born into other-genderedness. A "we" and "they" situation is set up; the country of "we" tends to pull together against the country of "they." Whenever we human beings are confronted with otherness, we view it with suspicion and alarm. Carol Bly describes this response in her essay: we look outside ourselves for the enemy, for the tiger behind the wild rose bush.

The voices that rise out of the poems and essays in these pages are the voices of human beings confronting their gendered condition. At their worst, the gender grievances, real and imagined, generate bewilderment, confusion, pain, hatred, and guilt. They drive us to teeth-clenching hostility, to scorn and contempt for the other. They sadden us with the grief that comes from any failure of communication, leaving us isolated from the other.

Unlike the indigo hamlet, we human beings will not know with every strand of our RNA what it is to be both male and female. Scott R. Sanders's essay, "The Men We Carry in Our Minds," is a good reminder that we must try to simulate the knowledge that comes from identity with the keenest imagination and the most sympathetic insight we are capable of, to give honor to what is different, recognizing that it is, nonetheless, the stuff of life.

The authors of a recent textbook, *Molecular Biology of the Cell*, address the question in a very basic way: "The machinery of sexual reproduction is elaborate, and the resources spent on it are large. What benefits does it bring and why did it evolve?" *Yes, indeed, the machinery is elaborate, and the emotional resources expended on it are enormous. Why not, like the hydra, bud off a complete offspring, or like the marine worm, split in two and regenerate the other half?* The answer, in biological terms, is that sexual reproduction gives us an evolutionary edge over the amoeba.

Asexual reproduction gives rise to offspring that are genetically identical to the parent offspring. Sexual reproduction produces *unpredictably dissimilar* offspring, individuals with novel assortments of genes, individuals who can adapt to a changing environment, because it involves the mixing and recombining of genes. In other words, it takes individuals of different genders to provide fresh genetic combinations, to provide novelty of a useful and beneficial sort that establishes favorable variants in a species. The painfulness and ecstasy of our gendered human state are translated in our chromosomes into complex possibilities for our species to surprise itself, to surpass itself. If it can manage to survive itself.

SHAKING THE BONES

Volume 5, Number 3, Fall 1984

English Skeleton: What do you suppose they mean by it—Shaking the Bones? Sounds violent to me.

American Skeleton: It's a colloquialism: it means move, dance, go for it, as in, "Shake them bones."

English Skeleton: So, by inference, it might mean inviting or confronting change.

American Skeleton: Sure. There's an excerpt from a Jon Hassler novel about a woman who decides, at the age of sixty-eight, to make a dramatic change in her life.

Latin American Skeleton: And why not? If we don't shake our own bones once in a while, life has a way of doing it for us.

German Skeleton: Vigorously!

English Skeleton: In order that we wake up. In order that we become aware of ourselves and what we're doing.

German Skeleton: So that we notice the dance each of us is dancing on the head of our own particular pin!

Latin American Skeleton: It is just because we are so separate that I was struck by the collaboration between the two poets Cardona-Hine and Hughes; it is a most delicate dance, the dance of partners who are able to respond to one another's subtlest signals, catch each other's moods and rhythms.

A breeze blowing through one of her poems moves a leaf in his.

English Skeleton: Sometimes, though, it takes a circumstance as large as history to force us to move.

Latin American Skeleton: Movement becomes survival.

English Skeleton: Bruchac makes that point in his essay. His Abenaki ancestors had the ability to keep moving, to keep changing, to disappear, and to survive.

English Skeleton: The rabbit-in-headlight syndrome.

Latin American Skeleton: That is why you shunt away the old, I suppose, because they are reminders of coming decline and disappearance.

American Skeleton: I find it strange that people are willing to exchange rather intimate confidences about their love lives, and even (!) about money, but that it upsets them to talk about the one subject they all have in common—their own impending death.

English Skeleton: You have no history of talking about death. You've been too concerned about making progress, about shooting off into space. And, of course, it makes poor ad copy.

German Skeleton: No tradition of memento mori, "Remember that you must die." In medieval times, people were always looking at the skull and crossbones, the emblems of mortality.

English Skeleton: Everyone accepted the idea that this world was a penitential journey of disease and pain, salted with tears, and that death was the gateway to an everlasting world.

German Skeleton: Or punishment.

American Skeleton: It's quite different now. Death used to be, as Ernest Becker puts it, "the ultimate promotion." When the concept of an afterlife fell into doubt, death became a big zero.

German Skeleton: A man's death used to be considered the natural crown of his life. Montaigne writes that "if we have lived steadfastly and calmly, we shall know how to die in the same way. Among the many duties of knowing how to live is this article of knowing how to die."

English Skeleton: Exactly. "Men must endure / Their going hence, even as their coming hither, / Ripeness is all."

American Skeleton: *King Lear, V, ii.* Well and good, but what about a culture that doesn't have any of the paraphernalia of Christian stoicism? We don't even have a native image for death.

Latin American Skeleton: Death, the consoler of the sick and wretched.

English Skeleton: The skeleton with the hourglass.

German Skeleton: The skeleton with the scythe. The grim reaper.

American Skeleton: We have the Baby New Year and the Easter Bunny and Santa Claus. The only image of death I can think of is the undertaker's polished limo.

German Skeleton: Death in his suit of bones was a familiar image throughout European art and folklore. There were thousands of representations. Hans Holbein's "Dance of Death" figures were probably the most famous—pictures of Death coming for the emperor, the ploughboy, the kitchen wench.

Latin American Skeleton: It helps people to recognize that death makes no exceptions. We have a *cuento* of a poor woodcutter who shares his meal with a death who comes to him in the guise of Dona Sebastiana. He tells her, "You are welcome to share my food, and I'll tell you why. You don't play favorites with the wealthy because of their money or with the beautiful because of their beauty, nor do you play favorites with the ugly or the young. No, you treat us all equally."

American Skeleton: We don't generally have that playfulness, or the feeling of familiarity toward the subject. Although there are exceptions, like Allen Ginsberg's *First Blues*. There's a song called, "Hey Father Death" that I found really touching without quite knowing why. It begins:

Hey, Father Death, I'm flying home
Hey poor man, you're all alone
Hey old daddy, I know where I'm going

Father Death, don't cry any more
Mama's there, underneath the floor
Brother Death, please mind the store

O Old Auntie Death, don't hide your bones
O Old Uncle Death, I hear your groans
O Sister Death, how sweet your moans

O Children Deaths, go breath your breaths
Sobbing breaths will ease your Deaths
Pain is gone, tears take the rest

Genius Death, your art is done
Lover Death, your body's gone
Father Death, I'm coming home

Guru Death, your words are true
Teacher Death, I do thank you
For inspiring, me to this Blues . . .

Latin American Skeleton: That is closer to our way of thinking.

American Skeleton: Ginsberg wrote that on his way home to his father's funeral.

German Skeleton: It acknowledges a closeness to death, but also there is a playfulness.

Latin American Skeleton: The playfulness is important. I would say that humor and familiarity help us to comprehend. We have fiestas in which dancers—who are shaking their bones—are wearing death masks. The deaths flirt and dance; it is part of the occasion.

English Skeleton: It deserves much talk, much more common talk. Because death points us back to life. How to live it well enough that leaving is all right, really.

American Skeleton: "Ripeness is all?"

English Skeleton: Yes, "the readiness is all."

American Skeleton: *Hamlet, V, ii.* Shaking the bones is all—
or at least a lot.

Latin American Skeleton: And playfulness.

German Skeleton: So that's why they've begun and ended the
issue with a cartoon—

HEALING

Volume 6, Number 1, Winter 1985

Although it is fantastic, an object unlike anything one has encountered before, the mask in the photo on the opposite page is faithful to the memory of a thing seen in a dream or read of in a story so deep and old that its source is buried. This image of a face adorned with medallions of silver, tin, and brass is a Mexican mask of miracles. Before entering the church, the visitor buys from a vendor the charm that symbolizes the miracle needed, for eye or hand or heart or other sick bodily part. Kneeling before the altar, the visitor pins a charm to a cloth spread for that purpose and offers up a prayer for healing to take place. The supplicant plays an active role; the miracle will not come to pass without the personal intervention.

To participate in healing seems to be a natural, creative human desire. Just as each of us secretly believes that he or she has a book to write, if given the opportunity, each of us has the desire to be a healer. Yet because we have given responsibility for healing into the trained hands of professionals—a reasonable and desirable thing in itself—individuals have forgotten their right to be part of the healing process.

The hospital visitor often concludes that she or he is a nonperson, waiting in vain for information from those too busy to give it, and recognizes that she or he is being asked to deposit the flowers (magazine, cologne, box of chocolates), say a few perfunctory words, and get out. The hospital patient, for his or her own good, is the object of scrutiny and treatment and, like most objects, is present to be acted upon. The shutting out of human interaction is the result of the inaccurate diagnosis that scientific treatment means eliminating the role of personal contact in human well-being. Only the hospice—where medical treatment is primarily used to the keep the patient free of pain—recognizes the importance of human touch and love, both for the patient and for those who wish to comfort and support the patient. As economic pressures force hospitals into greater competition for clients, all of us would benefit if hospitals assumed a stance that went beyond the merely efficient.

A miracle is rare, immediate, dramatic, and emotionally satisfying, which is why miracles are the source of songs, stories, and tabloid headlines. Ordinary healing, on the other hand, is a slow process with results that are often barely perceptible: the nailbed regrows, but that is not glamorous; no one wants to hear about it. Ordinary healing begins with pain and, often, continues with pain. Inside the pain, healing is the kernel that, to our surprise, is revealed when the pain falls away. Furthermore, healing is a lifetime occupation. Our bodies are always in a steady state of breakdown and repair. When the body fails to accomplish healing, it fails to keep on living. The body repeats the regenerative process over and over again, as must the psyche.

Being wounded and ill shows us our mortality, our frightening fragility. Ernest Becker comments in *The Denial of Death* that we turn our back on the pain of our mortality and hide the knowledge of it from ourselves in every way imaginable. As a nation, we are addicted to unreality. As individuals, we narcotize ourselves with our work and our play. We do our best to forget our own pain, and certainly we don't want to know much about anybody else's, especially if knowing means that we might have to do something about it. The graphic representation of pain and violence on television and the sight of starving children on the evening news provoke the same nonresponse and are in themselves narcotizing.

Perhaps we need, consciously, to increase our pain tolerance, to toughen up enough to look so that we can do more than look. One cannot even ask for a miracle without knowing that a miracle is needed. And for the tough, ongoing job of repair and regeneration to keep the body politic alive, a miracle is not enough.

EMPOWERMENT

Volume 6, Number 2, Spring/Summer 1985

A friend said that her childhood ended when she was twelve, the day she couldn't stop her mother from drowning the puppies the family dog had whelped under the porch. She cried and begged and promised to find homes for them. Her mother, dismissing her pleas, said, "This will save a whole lot of trouble."

It is bitter to lack the power—or to feel that you lack it—to defeat what you believe to be cruel or evil and thus to become an unwilling accomplice to the acts of others.

A child is especially vulnerable to feelings of helplessness, to seeing herself as the mute and powerless object acted upon, a perception David Mura explores in his examination of the relationship between powerlessness and abuse in "A Male Grief: Notes on Pornography and Addiction."

School rarely addresses a child's need to become an effective being. In fact, the function of much early education is to squeeze a child's energy and imagination into a form convenient for adult caretakers; the first few grades keep a child seated at a desk most of the day with the same intention as that in training a colt to saddle and bridle, to be passive and controllable. Even now, after more than a century of close attention to the education of children, recognizing the immense potential a young human being has for learning, education is still a matter of information ingestion and regurgitation rather than of developing a child's native abilities to imagine, to assess, and to make decisions.

Children learn very soon that it is politically wise to do what they are told, that it is *easier* not to make a fuss or to argue with an adult. More ominous still, they acquire the strange notion that others (teachers? Parents? An Olympian government? The Wizard of Oz?) know better than they do what is right, and that these others will fix whatever may be wrong in personal or public life.

Most of us remain the dutiful and obedient children of our training. Authoritarian governments recognize the value of imposing habits of obedience and passivity on its citizens. Most of us carry out orders, even loathsome ones, if the orders are signed and stamped with the seal of authority. We actually become angry with those who take a wrench to the smooth processing of policy, just as we are disgusted with the school troublemaker who disrupts the class and has to be sent to the principal's office. A society of free people, however, cannot hope to avoid the irritating, frustrating inconvenience of dissent, nor can such a society *afford* to avoid it.

Power-seeking has a bad reputation: only dictators or demagogues are presumed to be interested in acquiring power, their purpose being to exploit and enslave others. The truth is that the exercise of *personal* power—power to make our ideals actual—is as basic a necessity for human beings as eating or sleeping. We want to acquit ourselves decently and honorably. We want to have some measure of control over our lives. Yet our conditioning makes us embarrassed at the idea of seeming to want to control or influence. We prefer to be thought of as polite, good-natured, and cooperative rather than assume the responsibility that goes with having desires and dreams, so it is not surprising that much of the time we feel bested—by people, by circumstance, or by forces over which we seem to have no hope of control. It is not surprising that this reluctance to wield power "keeps us in our place" when we are children, a trait that prevents us from interfering with bad governance when we are adults.

Where there is no feeling of empowerment, there is no hope of making a difference. Without empowerment, the idealist becomes a cynic or a chronic malcontent or, despairing of change, a revolutionary. Because we are psychically blind to the power that belongs to each of us, we labor at the mill wearing the shackles we ourselves have forged, a failure of the imagination that Michael Kincaid addresses in the essay "Return to Power."

Perhaps what we need is an Outward Bound of the mind, programs that will teach children to appreciate the hostility and challenge of their environment and train them in thinking and feeling so that they may deal with that environment capably. The old apprentice, journeyman, master system of training might have good application here. Children would learn under the protection and guidance of mentors; after that, they would be encouraged to think and study independently, assessing their progress in conversations with fellow learners and mentors. As things stand now, this kind of learning process does not usually begin until the last few years of college, when it is often too late to develop either independent thinking or initiative. Such studies ought to begin in kindergarten.

One of the jobs for the mentor-teacher would be to suggest and organize reading materials, stories and poems and essays for student readings, and to cite, as Michael True has done in his essay "The Uses of Power," the seekers of truth and justice who find a way to be neither a victim nor a master, who use their personal power on behalf of others.

Myths and fairy tales and good children's books have always helped us to see that the world is a difficult place where heroic action is necessary. Walter de la Mare writes in *The Three Royal Monkeys*, "There was work to be done and brave hearts must take courage, else sorrow and trouble would be nothing but evil." That vision has helped children and adults survive their circumstances in the knowledge that others have drawn the sword out of the stone and have freed themselves when they were victims or slaves.

As a society, we have grown out of Nietzsche's nineteenth-century social Darwinism; we no longer believe that some are destined to be masters and most to be slaves. We find that idea not only repugnant but outdated, not because human beings have lost their will to power—which Nietzche calls "the will to life"—but because we have evolved to the point where we recognize that cooperative and collaborative power is the need of the future, a future in which each individual feels empowered to take part.

MAGIC

Volume 6, Number 3, Fall 1985

"As Goethe put it, we must plunge into experience and then reflect
on the meaning of it. All reflection and no plunging drives us mad;
all plunging and no reflection, and we are brutes."

—ERNEST BECKER, *THE DENIAL OF DEATH*

As Houdini would have agreed, stage magic has little to do with the
practice of magical arts. Thomas Cassidy's visual essay, "Suspended
without Wires," is a delightful overview of some of the highlights of
professional stage magic in which the magician seeks to engender the
willing suspension of disbelief in his audience by careful preparation
of the illusion and by dazzling showmanship. By contrast, in the se-
cretive, taboo-filled magic of most cultures, marked by the incanta-
tion of spells and the performance of rites, the performer is simply
the instrument of the magic.

The desire to believe in and make use of magic is rooted deep
in human beings; that desire is vigorous, local, and perennial, like
the herbs that practitioners often use, and it is common everywhere. Developing cultures routinely use magic to supplement
practical experiences: thus, in addition to penning up the cattle, a
guard is posted to alert the rest to an attack by wild dogs. And, in
the same spirit of practicality, the shaman is asked to surround the

corral with a spell to protect the cattle from the malignant spirits of the woods.

Generally, as knowledge systems develop, the practice of magic wanes; the impetus is always there, though, and in times of change, or stress, or hopelessness, an eruption of magic of some kind occurs, because magic is one response to impossible situations, an attempt to turn the world to one's will. As Sir James Frazer has noted, magic is an art in which theory and dogma are translated into action to subvert or turn aside the normal operations of the laws of nature; thus, the making of magic has often been one response of an oppressed group, a way of countering brute force in an unequal struggle by asking for help from nonhuman sources.

Makers of magic trade in several real commodities: human dissatisfaction and the desire to probe beyond what is known. There are times when we feel that the principles of physics and chemistry can be sidestepped—or wriggled out of, just as Houdini escaped from a straitjacket or chains and handcuffs, or a sealed steel milk can. It's a question of finding the way.

In our dreams and daydreams, we ourselves are magical—we can fly, we can make ourselves invisible, we can catch bullets in our hands—and generally venture beyond the common sense of what the culture accepts as true and reasonable.

Between waking and sleeping, in what has been called by some a trance state, mental activity is detached from its ordinary connections. In that limbo state, we are true amphibians. So much seems possible, so much knowable. We experience insights that make the clearest sense; we understand how to resolve the most riveting dilemmas. Some rich amalgam of emotion and reflection is fused—little of which survives the shock of the leap back to the culture of the waking world. Shakespeare expresses that bewildering sense of loss with humor and sadness in *A Midsummer Night's Dream* when Bottom tries to put his strange "dream" into words:

> *"I have had a most rare vision. I have had a dream past the wit of man to see what dream it was. Man is but an ass if he go about to expound this dream. . . ."*

The visions of the entranced—and almost everyone has had a flash of this feeling—seem to offer subjective evidence that the world we live in is only one possible kind of reality, and that our knowledge of it is limited by our equipment to perceive and to analyze. At such moments, the universe seems richer and more complex than we are able to express. But it is human to persist. Our language, imperfect and rigid in the face of the subtlety, nuance, and variety of sensation and thought, is still the most supple and versatile tool of our humanity. Dr. Bronislaw Malinowski writes that every act of magic consists of a spell, a rite, and an officiator, and that the spell is the outstanding part of the magical art, making use of metaphor and simile freely, as well as devising formulas of words to produce the desired magic. Michael Kincaid's essay in this issue explores the immense potential language gives us to recreate the world, to make our spells, to uncover our own power.

After the deadline for submissions had passed, we received a poem from Patricia Monaghan of Fairbanks, Alaska, that we decided to print in this preface. "She Hexes Newscasters" demonstrates one strong reason why the longing to make magic will never disappear from human impulse:

She Hexes Newscasters

What else could I do? For weeks
It has been one intolerable
Word after another, war and
War and war again and it seemed

So easy. Songs sprayed from
Their mouths, automatic carols:
Praise for the caliber of
Clouds and the blue shrapnel
Sky, the bombardment of the
Rain, praise for the maneuvers
Of finches and ravens, praise—

It is not enough, even though
It is my strongest spell, making
Beauty out of words. I
Repeat it, I repeat it
Nightly, I burn blue
Candles just to keep them
Singing. Oh, I want real power:

That soldiers, aiming at men's
Hearts, see into them and stop,
That presidents invoke old
Powers—earth and wind and
All their deputies—that
Generals sit before their maps
Telling rapt stories of the dawn.

LIMITS

Volume 7, Number 1, Winter 1986

*"For if thought is like the keyboard of a piano, divided into so
many notes, or like the alphabet is ranged in twenty-six letters
all in order, then his [Mr. Ramsay's] splendid mind had no sort
of difficulty in running over those letters one by one, firmly and
accurately, until it had reached, say, the letter Q. He reached
Q. . . . But after Q? What comes next? After Q there are a number of letters the last of which is scarcely visible to mortal eyes, but
glimmers red in the distance. Z is only reached once by one man
in a generation. Still, if he could reach R it would be something.
Here at least was Q."*

What prevents Mr. Ramsay from reaching R? Angels dancing on
the pin of earth? Preconceptions whose existence he will never
recognize?

In her magnificent novel *To the Lighthouse*, Virginia Woolf describes Mr. Ramsay's pursuit of thought in terms of exploration;
Mr. Ramsay is imagined as the leader of an expeditionary force:

*"Qualities that would have saved a ship's company exposed on a
broiling sea with six biscuits and a flask of water—endurance
and justice, foresight, devotion, skill, came to his help. R is
then—what is R?*

A shutter, like the leathern eyelid of a lizard, flickered over the intensity of his gaze and obscured the letter R. In that flash of darkness he heard people saying—he was a failure—that R was beyond him. He would never reach R. On to R, once more. R—"

The flash of darkness, the blinking off of intense intellectual abstraction, which Woolf shows us as provoking Mr. Ramsay's intense shame, might have provided an insight or an opportunity for meditation or speculation for a different kind of man. But Mr. Ramsay's mind, his splendid mind, was trained for restless and relentless questing, as were the minds of British explorers and colonizers of the nineteenth century.

Kirkpatrick Sale's essay, "Bound to Glory," traces the story of a restless man from another culture that did not respect the constraints of the natural world, a culture whose ethos was exploitation and conquest. "Bound to Glory" is an indictment of a society that has always had difficulty in telling the true from the false paradise.

Societies that believe thought is a linear track are uncomfortable about the idea that after Z there is, perhaps, another alphabet, or quite different modes of structuring thought. Such societies tend to be goal oriented and interested more in results than in observations.

Historically, we Americans have crossed distances and sought frontiers. Our nineteenth-century emblem of progress, the railroad, was a linear metal road to span a continent and collect its resources. The express train crossing the plains at a furious clip was a thrilling embodiment of the idea that our society was going somewhere and getting there fast. Part of its intellectual baggage was the idea of manifest destiny (it's all ours), the idea that it was all right to be grabby if you could get away with it, and the conviction that it was un-American to be limited in the use of land or food or water.

Science has been our twentieth-century frontier. We have made such brilliant practical application of the leaps of knowledge in mathematics and physics and chemistry that we are gifted with a remarkable expansion of comfort and information distribution as well as extraordinary military capability, a mixed bag of blessings. This century has also brought the gift of the social sciences, offering for the first time insights into human motivation and behavior, insights that transcend geographical boundaries.

We are gradually recognizing that what we learn from the social sciences has relevance to our use of technological information; we are also learning that having the capability to implement a technology does not necessarily mean we should. Technology is the express train of our century, our emblem of going somewhere and getting there fast. What seems obvious, but has not been attended to, is the idea that those at the throttle should have some training in human values.

Carol Bly's essay, "Bad Government and Silly Literature," urges writers to move past the limits of present literary convention, to add that concern for human values to their writing. The essay invites writers of fiction to consider whether they are truthfully representing their world when they create characters who live in a moral and political vacuum. Bly's thrust is to convince writers that expressing their worldview in their fiction and incorporating valuable and hope-giving concepts pioneered by the social sciences can result in powerful, visionary writing.

Virginia Woolf sets before us the painful rigidity of the intellectual explorer who lacks the feeling of being human, of being humane, exposing to the reader the great and grave difference between merely possessing information and having true understanding. In the Renaissance, people believed that the difference between men and angels was that men were capable only of reason, angels of understanding. Intellectual exploration of all kinds—especially scientific and technological—needs to be accompanied by a regard for human values, so that we not only know but understand. To respect and uphold human values, to understand, is a necessity, our necessary angel. In Wallace Stevens's words: "I am the necessary angel of earth / Since in my sight you see the earth again, / cleared of its stubborn, man-locked set."

Only in the presence of the necessary angel should we allow ourselves to say: On then, on to R.

SEEING BETTER

Volume 7, Number 2, Spring/Summer 1986

Because we learn better through image than through abstraction, our myths and legends are picture-stories of quest. This issue is a gathering of photographs and writing about sight and insight.

We've been living with the photographs on these pages for a while; they are the survivors of a tough winnowing. They've been dealt out onto every possible surface; our desks and tables are buried under images. We've walked around them; stopped and thought about them one by one. We've compared them, a couple at a time, considering which might be combined on the page in groupings that would respect the integrity of the individual photograph but be appropriate and energizing combined with others.

We've asked one another: what's the common denominator? And we've decided that was not the right question. We wanted diversity, different photographic styles, a variety of subjects, to approach the more difficult question: how do these photographs enable a viewer to see some fragment of the world with clearer vision?

Sometimes a photograph captures what is deeply, powerfully familiar—a dog settled guiltily in a comfortable chair, a woman with her hands placed in exasperation on her hips—and our recognition rushes to meet and embrace the image. Sometime a photographic technique can turn the familiar form of a tree into feathers of blooming light, revising, in an instant, the definition of a tree.

Contemporary photographs that document the survival of tradition in China assume new meaning now when China is hurrying to embrace Western customs.

A costumed face dramatically lit and shot close up is a new landscape. Photographs of men's hands, almost as expressive as faces, are clues to self-definition. "Rocks resist being moved, and soul resists seeing itself as other people see it," Robert Bly says in "Placing Rocks in a Stream." Certain photographs are soul catchers.

We considered for a long time the placement of poems with photographs. A few poems in this issue, those by Margot Kriel Galt and Christina Baldwin, were written about the photographs that accompany them. Except for these, no poem is intended as a direct comment on a photograph. No photograph is to be thought of as directly illustrative of a poem. Their flights are as different as a bird's is from a cloud's, but they move over the same deep water.

Carolyn Forché and Harry Mattison talk about the paths imaginative truth can take, in their introductory essay to "So Much Home," from the Iron Range Community Documentary Project. From the beginning, "the writers who had come to listen, the photographers who had come to lift their camera at the exact moment of human revelation and regard" recognized that although they are documenting the same people and the same land, the insights of the camera might have a different texture, a different focus than those offered by words. Their work included learning to see themselves in "the tenuous, delicate, and intuitive work of self-perception" and making sure "that every image, visual and verbal, be the product of respectful human contact."

The joint work of Timothy Francisco and Patricia Weaver Francisco, the photographer and the writer of "Tarascan Faces," also approaches, with delicacy and consideration, a people who rarely see themselves, to document something that is becoming more and more unusual: faces that do not look into mirrors, faces that have not learned to assume an automatic pose, faces that reflect the inner being.

We quite literally must learn to see. A newborn is aware only of movement and light intensity. The work that earned Karl Pribam a

Nobel Prize for the hologram in 1971 showed that visual information is radically modified before it reaches the visual cortex. Patterns of visual recognition feed forward, along with remembered forms. Seen images are compared with stored memories, interests, and expectations. These collide with the visual information in an interference pattern.

It's truly difficult, therefore, to "see better," because we tend not to see *other* than what we have already learned to recognize. This system of repeated references makes seeing easier; it also makes it easier to convince the public to prefer an actor or a headache remedy by showing us an image in print or on film or on videotape, over and over again.

Photographer Nancy Burson uses our familiarity as viewers of such recurrent images in her patient, ingenious work with computer digital image processing. Burson's composite photographs jolt the viewer's expectations with an image that is almost familiar, that resembles but isn't the image we expect.

Her 1983 photograph, *Big Brother*, is a composite of Adolf Hitler, Benito Mussolini, Joseph Stalin, Mao Tse-tung, and the Ayatollah Khomeini. The result is a face that, though it has never existed, is disturbingly, elusively known to us.

Burson's composites, made with computer scientists David Karmich and Richard Carling, are a union of art and science, visions that use the conventional photograph as raw material in providing visual answers to "what if" questions. A composite called *Androgyny* synthesizes six male and six female faces; *Lion/Lamb* is an intriguing candidate for a medieval bestiary, the equal commingling of the facial structure of a lion and a lamb.

New photographic technology has the potential, like any other tool, to enslave us, to bamboozle us, or to force us to look harder at our visual preconceptions, the images that shape our lives and people our myths.

TRAVEL: THERE AND BACK AGAIN

Volume 7, Number 3, Fall 1986

A flight to Oz in the gut of a tornado? A pilgrimage to destroy
Sauron's ring in the Cracks of Doom? A child taking the school bus
alone on the first day of kindergarten is making that kind of heroic
journey. Travel is the experience of leaving the safety of home, of
divorcing the familiar. To willingly become a stranger in a strange
land is to learn something about one's self.

Not only is *National Geographic* the most popular magazine in
the world but it is also the most difficult (for me) to throw away.
We go back to those pages again and again to pore over the photographs, substitutes for the trips we can't afford to take, destinations
that will never be printed on our itineraries. Producers make films on
location in exotic places because they take advantage of our eagerness
for a glimpse of Khartoum or Bora Bora. Our desire to have a valid
insight into the lives of others is whetted by glossy photographs and
the Technicolor backdrops of other countries, but the experience of
travel can only be suggested, not satisfied, by these visuals.

That experience involves the texture of the light, the smells of
markets and cafes, the sounds of voices speaking words in an unfamiliar language. Good writing about even the most familiar place
produces some of the extraordinary insights and recognitions we
hope to experience when we travel. Putting together this issue, we
made vicarious visits to Zimbabwe, the Italian Riviera, a Caribbean

island, Leningrad, Tokyo, Swede Prairie Township in Minnesota, Machu Picchu, Madera Canyon, Mt. Wrightson, Memphis, the California desert, a small Irish town, a road in the middle of Ohio, the shah's palace in Tehran, and a hotel in Washington, DC, to name only some of the stops on the journey.

The heroine of Tess Gallagher's haunting story, "Girls," travels to see a woman who was an essential part of her youth: "What was she doing here, she wondered, in this woman's bed in a city far from her own home?" She has made a journey in the hope of finding her girlhood self again, reflected in the eyes of a friend long missing from her life. Once, "they had tried on each other's clothes and shared letters from home. But this was the future and she had come here alone."

Nora Reza also shares vivid memories of the past, of a Tehran she remembers from childhood, a culture she knew intimately as a child and returned to as a young woman; her description of the Tehran that existed before the toppling of the shah is a glimpse into a society that is not as dead as the empires of ancient Persia.

Beth Siebert's essay, "Go," produces the heightened awareness of a trip taken alone. Such a trip makes one conscious of each new face, each scene witnessed. Siebert catches the exultation of being an anonymous observer. She also describes the anxiety of being unknown and, literally, out of place. That edgy feeling of being an outsider, of not knowing the lingo or the terrain, results in a physical and emotional sensitivity that notes and records differences the arrangement of food on a plate or in the mode of dress. At first, one looks for the reassurance of the familiar, but after a while one recognizes that differences are not necessarily threatening. Then one truly begins to savor travel, to find out what one lacks and is looking for, and what "home" really means. That knowledge allows one to make common cause with the world and to say of it, as Siebert does: "This is my home. This is my family. These are my friends."

The work in this issue demonstrates that the insights of travel are as available on the bus heading home as in the most unfamiliar terrain. The essential travel accessories are open eyes and the willingness to know and to be known by others. And to travel without sensitivity and imagination is to go nowhere at all.

Traveling On: Milkweed Editions

This is the last issue of the *Milkweed Chronicle*. To make this issue the last will enable us to commit our time and energy into acquiring, editing, designing, publishing, marketing, and distributing Milkweed Editions books.

This decision was not arrived at without considerable discussion. The *Chronicle* has been the focus of our attention for the past seven years. We've loved the work, experimenting with format, choosing each issue's content. We've had the satisfaction of printing fine work by a large number of writers and visual artists, and of being the first publication credit for many of them.

There is no "set" page of the *Chronicle*; the making of each issue is a hands-on, time-consuming process that involves counterpointing poems, juxtaposing words and images, and creating a visual flow throughout the issue that encourages browsing and then a reading and, we have hoped, a rereading. It's fun of the most satisfying kind; we will miss it very much.

We've been lucky in our readership. Many of you have been readers from our first years of publishing the *Chronicle*. You have stayed with us as we took up challenges of varying kinds: we have published three-hundred-line poems, changed from a tabloid format, presented unusual collaborations, added a separate cover, tried new papers and typefaces, and printed whole chapbooks in an issue. We have appreciated your letters of commentary. Even a letter of violent disagreement was welcome to us because it meant that the work in the issue was being read and responded to.

Since we began publishing books, we have found ourselves increasingly drawn by projects we want to attempt, and by an ever-increasing number of book-length manuscripts we'd like to be able to publish. We've also found ourselves consistently behind the eight ball: understaffed and out of time. We knew that we had to make a choice. Fortunately, a small press is not a museum. The challenges change, the organization evolves.

Many of our goals and priorities remain: Milkweed Editions will carry on our commitment to providing opportunities for emerging writers and artists. Our anthologies, like *The Poet Dreaming in the Artist's House* and *This Sporting Life*, will always feature both emerging and recognized writers.

We plan to publish more fiction. The Milkweed National Fiction Prize will publicize our interest in attracting excellent manuscripts. Milkweed Editions will also begin a series of visual art books in late 1988. We are discussing various possible formats for these books with artists, art critics, and visual arts organizations.

Of course, we will continue our emphasis on collaborative work. It's our hope that the simultaneous publication of the limited edition and the trade edition of *Spillville* by Patricia Hampl and Steven Sorman will focus attention on the excitement and energy generated by collaboration.

The Thistle series of chapbook essays, initiated by Carol Bly's *Bad Government and Silly Literature*, will continue with the publication of David Mura's *A Male Grief: Notes on Pornography and Addiction*, an essay originally published in the *Chronicle* for which we've had numerous requests. We want to expand this series to publish thought-provoking essays about subjects of importance to our society.

We promise not to lose touch. Several times a year we'll send out a Milkweed newsletter to give you the first glimpse of what's forthcoming. We would like to hear your ideas about the sorts of books you think a literary small press should be tackling. Let us hear from you.

MILKWEED BOARD MEMBERS, 1980–2003

Philip Harder

*Judith K. Healey

Mary Hipp

Linda Hoeschler

David A. Houghtby

Richard Howell

George R. A. Johnson

Jane Johnston

Kathleen Jones

*Randy Lebedoff

Sally Lebedoff

Adam Lerner

Ann Lewis

*Dorothy K. Light

Charles Lukaszewski

Dustin Macgregor

Sally Macut

Chris Malacek

Paul Martinucci

Thomas Mason

Don McNeil

Mary Merrill

Mary Jane Miller

Herman J. Milligan, Jr.

Sheila Morgan

Diane Neimann

Robin Nelson

Ann Ness

Dan Odegard

Michael O'Shaughnessy

Allegra Parker

Edmund Phelps, Jr.

David W. Pratt

*Margaret Robinson Preska

Peter R. Reis

Sarah Dougherty Rekas

*Debbie Reynolds

Becky Rom

Cheryl Ryland

Jonathan Scoll

*Cynthia Snyder

Elly Sturgis

Celeste Taylor

Lynn Truesdell

Moira Turner

Joanne Von Blon

*Brenda Wehle

Dickinson Wiltz

Theodore Zorn

MILKWEED STAFF, 1980–2003

1980, 1981, 1982

Publisher, Editor, Emilie Buchwald
Publisher, Art Director, R. W. Scholes

Part-Time Staff

Business Manager, Laurie Lykken
(Spring/Summer 1980)
Business Director, Marilyn Heltzer
(Fall 1980–1982)
Bookkeeper: Ann Rest
Copy Editor: Denise Dreher
(Fall 1980–Winter 1981)
Volunteer, Marilyn Matthews

1983, 1984, 1985

Publisher, Editor, Emilie Buchwald
Publisher, Art Director, R. W. Scholes

Part-Time Staff

Business Manager, Paulette Bates
Alden
Subscription Manager, Deborah
Heltzer
Copy Editor, Mary Ellen Shaw
Public Relations, Lisa McLean
Bookkeeper, Mary Hipp
Assistant Subscription Manager,
Derek Phillips
Volunteer, Marilyn Matthews

1986

Publisher, Editor, Emilie Buchwald
Publisher, Art Director, R. W. Scholes
Managing Editor, Deborah Keenan
Business Manager, Steve Chase
Volunteer, Marilyn Matthews

1987

Publisher, Editor, Emilie Buchwald
Publisher, Art Director, R. W. Scholes
Managing Editor, Deborah Keenan
Business Manager, Steve Chase
Editorial Assistant, Roseann Lloyd
Volunteer, Marilyn Matthews

1988

Publisher, Editor, Emilie Buchwald
Publisher, Art Director, R. W. Scholes
Managing Editor, Deborah Keenan
Business Manager, Steve Chase
Editorial Assistant, Roseann Lloyd
Business Assistant, Mark Schultz
Volunteer, Marilyn Matthews

1989

Publisher, Editor, Emilie Buchwald
Publisher, Art Director, R. W. Scholes
Managing Editor, Deborah Keenan
Development Director, Teresa Bonner

Office Manager, Mark Schultz
Administrative Volunteer, Marilyn
  Matthews

1990

Publisher, Editor, Emilie Buchwald
Publisher, Art Director, R.W. Scholes
Marketing and Development
  Director, Teresa Bonner
Business Manager, Kathleen
  Martinson-Gibson
Administrative Assistant, Beryl B.
  Tanis
Administrative Volunteer, Marilyn
  Matthews

1991

Publisher, Editor, Emilie Buchwald
Publisher, Art Director, R.W. Scholes
Executive Director and Marketing
  Director, Teresa Bonner
Business Manager, Kathleen
  Martinson-Gibson
Development Director, Sue Jacob
Editorial Assistant, Fiona S. Grant
Administrative Assistant, Beryl B.
  Tanis
Administrative Volunteer, Marilyn
  Matthews

1992

Publisher, Editor, Emilie Buchwald
Publisher, Art Director, R.W. Scholes
Executive Director, Teresa Bonner
Business Manager, Kathleen
  Martinson-Gibson
Development and Community
  Relations, Ellen E. Watters
Copy Editor, Fiona S. Grant
Administrative Assistant, Beryl B.
  Tanis

Business Assistant, Caroline Kuebler
Administrative Volunteer, Marilyn
  Matthews

1993

Publisher, Editor, Emilie Buchwald
Publisher, Art Director, R.W. Scholes
Executive Director, Teresa Bonner
Financial Director, Diane M.
  Murphy
Production and Publicity Director,
  Arlinda Keeley
Development and Community
  Relations, Ellen E. Watters
Production Editor, Fiona S. Grant
Editorial Assistant, Scott Muskin
Office Manager, Beryl B. Tanis
Editorial Consultant, Brigitte Frase
Administrative Volunteer, Marilyn
  Matthews

1994

Publisher, CEO, Editor, Emilie
  Buchwald
Executive Director, COO, Teresa
  Bonner
Financial Director, Diane M. Murphy
Promotions and Publicity Director,
  Arlinda Keeley
Development and Community
  Relations, Ellen E. Watters
Assistant Editor, Fiona S. Grant
Editorial Assistant, Scott Muskin
Office Manager, Beryl B. Tanis
Editorial Consultant, Brigitte Frase
Administrative Volunteer, Marilyn
  Matthews

1995

Publisher, CEO, Editor, Emilie
  Buchwald

Executive Director, Gayle Peterson
Marketing and Sales Director, Bob
  Breck
Financial Director, Diane M.
  Murphy
Managing Editor, Beth Olson
Executive Editor, Molly McQuade
Editorial Assistant, Scott Muskin
Administrative Assistant, Laurie
  Buss
Office Manager, Intern Coordinator,
  Beryl B. Tanis
Editorial Consultant, Brigitte Frase
Administrative Volunteer, Marilyn
  Matthews

1996

Publisher, CEO, Editor, Emilie
  Buchwald
Executive Director, Gayle Peterson
Marketing and Sales Director, Bob
  Breck
Financial Director, Bonnie Nelson
Managing Editor, Beth Olson
Executive Editor, Molly McQuade
Editorial Assistant, Laurie Buss
Administrative Assistant, Elizabeth
  Cleveland
Office Manager, Intern Coordinator,
  Beryl B. Tanis
Editorial Consultant, Brigitte Frase
Administrative Volunteer, Marilyn
  Matthews

1997

Publisher, CEO, Editor, Emilie
  Buchwald
Executive Director, Sid Farrar
Marketing and Sales Director, Bob
  Breck
Finance Manager, Bonnie Nelson

Managing Editor, Beth Olson
Editorial Assistant, Laurie Buss
Production Assistant, Intern
  Coordinator, Elizabeth Cleveland
Marketing Assistant, Susan Doerr
Development Associate, Beryl
  Singleton Bissell
Administrative Assistant, Kristin
  Roessler
Editorial Consultant, Brigitte Frase
Administrative Volunteer, Marilyn
  Matthews

1998

Publisher, CEO, Editor, Emilie
  Buchwald
Executive Director, Sid Farrar
Marketing and Sales Director, Bob
  Breck
Finance Manager, Molly Elton
Managing Editor, Beth Olson
Editorial Assistant, Laurie Buss
Marketing Assistant, Susan Doerr
Development Associate, Beryl
  Singleton Bissell
Administrative Assistant, Kristin
  Roessler
Production Assistant, Anja Welsh
Editorial Consultants, Brigitte
  Frase, Christine Hepperman
Administrative Volunteer, Marilyn
  Matthews

1999

Publisher, CEO, Editor, Emilie
  Buchwald
Executive Director, Sid Farrar
Marketing and Sales Director,
  Hilary Reeves
Financial Manager, Molly Elton
Art and Design Editor, Beth Olson

Development Assistant, Intern
Coordinator, Emily Heynen
Production Editor, Laurie Buss
Editorial Assistant, Greg Larson
Publicist, Susan Doerr
Production Assistant, Anja Welsh
Editorial Consultant, Brigitte Frase
Administrative and Customer
Service Associate, Eric Norsted
Administrative Volunteers, Marilyn
Matthews, Laura Boeringa

2000

Publisher, CEO, Editor, Emilie
Buchwald
Executive Director, Sid Farrar
Marketing and Sales Director,
Hilary Reeves
Financial Manager, Molly Bromert
Managing Editor, Laurie Buss
Assistant Editor, Greg Larson
Publicist, Susan Doerr
Production Assistant, Anja Welsh
Art and Design Coordinator, Dale
Cooney
Web Coordinator, Erik Norsted
Marketing and Customer Service
Assistant, Elizabeth Cooper
Development Assistant, Dawn
Newstrom
Editorial Consultant, Brigitte Frase
Administrative Volunteers, Marilyn
Matthews, Laura Boeringa

2001–2002

Publisher, CEO, Editor, Emilie
Buchwald
Executive Director, Sid Farrar
Marketing and Sales Director,
Hilary Reeves

Financial Manager, Jennifer Mendoza
Managing Editor, Laurie Buss
Greg Larson, Assistant Editor
Art and Design Coordinator, Dale
Cooney
Production and Marketing
Assistant, Ben Barnhart
Publicist, Elizabeth Cooper
Web and Promotions Coordinator,
Erik Norsted
Development Assistant and Intern
Coordinator, Dawn Newstrom
Editorial Consultants, Brigitte Frase,
Scott Slovic, Sara St. Antoine
Administrative Volunteers, Marilyn
Matthews, Laura Boeringa

2003

Publisher, CEO, Editor, Emilie
Buchwald
Financial Director, Anita Poda
Moulton
Development Director, Mary
Rondeau Westra
Marketing and Sales Director,
Hilary Reeves
Managing Editor, Laurie Buss
Assistant Editor, Ben Barnhart
Art and Design Coordinator,
Christian Funfhausen
Publicist, Elizabeth Cooper
Financial Manager, Jennifer
Mendoza
Development Associate and Intern
Coordinator, Katie Clymer
Editorial Consultants, Brigitte
Frase, Debbie Meister, Scott
Slovic, Sara St. Antoine
Administrative Volunteer, Marilyn
Matthews

MILKWEED EDITIONS TITLES,
1984–2004

POETRY

Amichai, Yehuda
Amen, 1987
translated from the Hebrew by the
author and Ted Hughes, with a
foreword by Ted Hughes

Black, Ralph
Turning Over the Earth, 2000

Breckenridge, Jill
Civil Blood: Poems and Prose, 1986

**Burns, Ralph and Pfingston,
Roger**
Windy Tuesday Nights, 1985

Caddy, John
Eating the Sting, 1986
The Color of Mesabi Bones, 1989
*Morning Earth: Field Notes in
Poetry*, 2003

Chin, Marilyn
*The Phoenix Gone, The Terrace
Empty*, 1993

Dacey, Philip
The Man with Red Suspenders, 1986

Driscoll, Jack and Meissner, Bill
*Twin Sons of Different Mirrors:
Poems in Dialogue*, 1989

Glancy, Diane
One Age in a Dream, 1985

Goedicke, Patricia
*The Tongues We Speak: New and
Selected Poems*, 1989
Paul Bunyan's Bearskin, 1992
Invisible Horses, 1996

Gonzales, Angel
*Astonishing World: The Selected
Poems of Angel Gonzales 1956–1986*
translated by Steven Ford Brown
and Gutierrez Revuelta, 1993

Hamill, Sam and Garwood, Galen
Mandala, 1991

Hanson, Phebe
Sacred Hearts, 1986

Hasse, Margaret
In a Sheep's Eye, Darling, 1987

Hauge, Olav H.
Trusting Your Life to Water and
Eternity, 1987
translated from the Norwegian
by Robert Bly, with a foreword by
Robert Bly

Holm, Bill
Boxelder Bug Variations: A
Meditation on an Idea in
Language and Music, 1985, 1991
The Dead Get By with Everything,
1991
Playing the Black Piano, 2004

Humes, Harry
Butterfly Effect, 1999

Hyde, Lewis
This Error Is the Sign of Love, 1989

Keenan, Deborah
Good Heart, 2003

Keenan, Deborah and Moore, Jim
How We Missed Belgium, 1985

Moore, Jim
The Freedom of History, 1987, 1991
The Long Experience of Love, 1995

Neruda, Pablo
The House in the Sand, 1989
translated by Dennis Maloney and
Clark M. Zlotchew

Nordhaus, Jean
The Porcelain Apes of Moses
Mendelssohn, 2002

Paddock, Joe
Earth Tongues, 1985

Roberts, Len
Sweet Ones, 1987

Rogers, Pattiann
Firekeeper: New and Selected Poems,
1994
Eating Bread and Honey, 1997
Song of the World Becoming: New
and Collected Poems, 1981–2001, 2001

Sampson, Dennis
Forgiveness, 1990

Vance-Watkins, Lequita and
Mariko, Aritani, editors
White Flash, Black Rain, 1995

Vinz, Mark and Gudmanson,
Wayne
Minnesota Gothic, 1992

FICTION

Ardizzone, Tony
Larabi's Ox: Stories of Morocco, 1992

Birdsell, Sandra
Agassiz: A Novel in Stories, 1991
Katya, 2004

Bliss, Corinne Demas
What We Save for Last, 1992

Bly, Carol
Backbone, 1985
My Lord Bag of Rice: New and
Selected Stories, 2000

Bridal, Tessa
The Tree of Red Stars, 1997

Browder, Catherine
The Clay That Breathes: A Novella
and Stories, 1991

Brown, Rosellen
Street Games: A Neighborhood, 1991

Carpenter, William
A Keeper of Sheep, 1994

Dorner, Marjorie
Winter Roads, Summer Fields, 1992, 2000
Seasons of Sun and Rain, 2000

Drew, Eileen
Blue Taxis: Stories about Africa, 1989

Garber, Eugene
The Historian: Six Fantasies of the American Experience, 1993

Hawley, Ellen
Trip Sheets, 1998

Haynes, David
Somebody Else's Mama, 1995
Live at Five, 1996
All American Dream Dolls, 1997

Heath, William
The Children Bob Moses Led, 1995

Higgins, Joanna
The Importance of High Places: Stories and a Novella, 1993

Kalfus, Ken
Thirst, 1998
Pu-239 and Other Russian Fantasies, 1999

Kantner, Seth
Ordinary Wolves, 2004

Kaschnitz, Marie Luise
Circe's Mountain, 1989
translated by Lisel Mueller

Langley, Lee
Persistent Rumours, 1994
Distant Music, 2003

Lowell, Susan
Ganado Red: A Suite of Stories, 1987

McNeil, Jean
Hunting Down Home, 1999

Meyers, Margaret
Swimming in the Congo, 1995

O'Connor, Sheila
Tokens of Grace, 1990

Power, Susan
Roofwalker, 2002

Pritchett, Laura
Hells Bottom, Colorado, 2001

Rangel-Ribeiro, Victor
Tivolem, 1998

Rodriguez, Abraham, Jr.
The Boy Without a Flag: Tales of the South Bronx, 1992, 1999

Schweidel, David
Confidence of the Heart, 1995

Sidhwa, Bapsi
Cracking India, 1991
The Crow Eaters, 1992
An American Brat, 1995

Stanton, Maura
The Country I Come From, 1989

Stowell, Jim
Traveling Light, 1988

Straight, Susan
Aquaboogie, 1990

Sullivan, Faith
The Empress of One, 1996
What a Woman Must Do, 2002

Tharp, Tim
Falling Dark, 1999

Veltfort, Ruhama
The Promised Land, 1998

Watson, Larry
Montana 1948, 1993
Justice, 1994

FICTION + POETRY ANTHOLOGIES

Benedict, Elinor, editor
Passages North Anthology, 1993

Blossom, Laurel, editor
*Many Lights in Many Windows:
Twenty Years of Great Fiction
and Poetry from The Writers
Community*, 1997

Bonner, Barbara, editor
*Sacred Ground: Writings about
Home*, 1997

Bosselaar, Laure-Anne, editor
*Outsiders: Poems about Rebels, Exiles,
and Renegades*, 1995
*Urban Nature: Poems about Wildlife
in the City*, 1999

Brown, Kurt, editor
*Verse and Universe: Poems about
Science and Mathematics*, 1998

**Brown, Kurt and Bosselaar,
Laure-Anne,** editors
*Night Out: Poems about Hotels,
Motels, Restaurants and Bars*, 1997

**Buchwald, Emilie and Roston,
Ruth,** editors
*The Poet Dreaming in the Artist's
House*, 1984
*Mixed Voices: Contemporary Poems
about Music*, 1986
*This Sporting Life: Poems about
Sports and Games*, 1998

**Dorris, Michael and Buchwald,
Emilie,** editors
*The Most Wonderful Books: Writers
on Discovering the Pleasures of
Reading*, 1997

Gander, Forrest, editor
*Mouth to Mouth: Poems by Twelve
Contemporary Mexican Women*,
1993

Graves, Ken and Lipman, Eva,
editors
Ballroom, 1989

**Haynes, David and Landsman,
Julie,** editors
*Welcome to Your Life: Writings for
the Heart of Young America*, 1998

**Keenan, Deborah and Lloyd,
Roseann,** editors
*Looking for Home: Women Writing
about Exile*, 1990

Moore, Jim and Waterman, Cary,
editors
Minnesota Writes Poetry, 1987
COPUBLISHED WITH NODIN PRESS

**Sapinkopf, Lisa and Belev,
Georgi,** editors and translators
*Clay and Star: Contemporary
Bulgarian Poets*, 1992

Vance-Watkins, Lequita and
    Mariko, Aratini
*White Flash/Black Rain: Women of
    Japan Relive the Bomb*, 1995

NONFICTION

Bly, Carol
*Bad Government and Silly
    Literature: An Essay*, 1984
*The Passionate, Accurate Story:
    Making Your Heart's Truth into
    Literature*, 1990, 1998
*Changing the Bully Who Rules the
    World: Reading and Writing
    about Ethics*, 1996

Buchwald, Emilie, Fletcher,
    Pamela, and Roth, Martha,
    editors
Transforming a Rape Culture,
    1993
Transforming a Rape Culture,
    Revised Edition, 2004

Dorris, Michael
Rooms in the House of Stone, 1993

Francisco, Timothy and Weaver
    Francisco, Patricia
Village without Mirrors, 1989

Gershgoren, Sid and Peer, George
Through the Sky into the Lake,
    1991

Guest, Judith
The Mythic Family: An Essay, 1988

Hamill, Sam, translator
*The Art of Writing: Lu Chi's Wen
    Fu*, 1991, 2000

Hampl, Patricia and Sorman,
    Steven
Spillville, 1987
PAPERBACK AND LETTERPRESS
    EDITION

Hoffman, Marvin
*Chasing Hellhounds: A Teacher
    Learns from His Students*, 1996

Holm, Bill
*Coming Home Crazy: An Alphabet
    of China Essays*, 1990, 2000
*The Heart Can Be Filled Anywhere
    on Earth*, 1996, 2001
*Eccentric Islands: Travels Real and
    Imaginary*, 2000

Holub, Miroslav
*Shedding Life: Disease, Politics,
    and Other Human Conditions*,
    1997

Jones, Syl
Rescuing Little Roundhead, 1996

Kohl, Herbert
*I Won't Learn from You! The Role of
    Assent in Learning*, 1991

Landsman, Julie
*Basic Needs: A Year with Street Kids
    in a City School*, 1994
*Tips for Creating a Manageable
    Classroom: Understanding Your
    Students' Basic Needs*, 1994

Merrill, Christopher
*The Old Bridge: The Third Balkan
    War and the Age of the Refugee*,
    1995

Morrish, William R. and Brown, Catherine R.
Planning to Stay: Learning to See the Physical Features of Your Neighborhood, 1994, 2000

Mura, David
A Male Grief: Notes on Pornography and Addiction: An Essay, 1987

Roth, Martha
Arousal: Bodies and Pleasures, 1998

Stafford, Kim, editor
Every War Has Two Losers: William Stafford on Peace and War, 2003

Stoltenberg, John
What Makes Pornography "Sexy"? 1994

THE WORLD AS HOME

Bass, Rick
Brown Dog of the Yak: Essays on Art and Activism, 1999

Bruchac, Joseph
At the End of Ridge Road, 2004

Buchwald, Emilie, editor
Toward the Livable City, 2003

Butler, Tom, editor
Wild Earth: Wild Ideas for a World Out of Balance, 2002

Cerulean, Susan, editor
The Book of the Everglades, 2002
translated by Gayle Wurst

Collet, Anne
Swimming with Giants: My Encounters with Whales, Dolphins, and Seals, 2000

Daniel, John
Winter Creek: One Writer's Natural History, 2002

Daum, Ann
The Prairie in Her Eyes, 2001

Deming, Alison Hawthorne
Writing the Sacred into the Real, 2001

Deming, Alison Hawthorne and Savoy, Lauret, editors
The Colors of Nature: Culture, Identity, and the Natural World, 2002

Elder, John
The Frog Run: Words and Wildness in the Vermont Woods, 2002

Gruchow, Paul
Grass Roots: The Universe of Home, 1995
Boundary Waters: The Grace of the Wild, 1997
The Necessity of Empty Places, 1999

Hopes, David Brendan
A Sense of the Morning: Field Notes of a Born Observer, 1999
Birdsongs of the Mesozoic, 2004

Kittredge, William
Taking Care: Thoughts on Storytelling and Belief, 1999

Lentfer, Hank and Servid, Carolyn, compilers
Arctic Refuge: A Circle of Testimony, 2001

Lyon, Thomas J.
This Incomparable Land: A Guide to American Nature Writing, Revised Edition, 2001

McQuay, Peri Phillips
*A Wing in the Door: Life with a
Red-Tailed Hawk,* 2001

Moore, Kathleen Dean
The Pine Island Paradox, 2004

Nabhan, Gary Paul
*Cross-Pollinations: The Marriage of
Science and Poetry,* 2003

Nichols, John
*An American Child Supreme:
The Education of a Liberation
Ecologist,* 2001

O'Reilley, Mary Rose
*The Barn at the End of the World:
The Apprenticeship of a Quaker,
Buddhist Shepherd,* 2000

Pyle, Robert Michael
*Walking the High Ridge: Life As
Field Trip,* 2000

Ray, Janisse
Ecology of a Cracker Childhood, 1999
Wild Card Quilt, 2003

Rogers, Pattiann
*The Dream of the Marsh Wren:
Writing As Reciprocal Creation,*
1999

Sanders, Scott Russell
The Country of Language, 1999

Scherer, Migael
*Back Under Sail: Recovering the
Spirit of Adventure,* 2003

Servid, Carolyn
*Of Landscape and Longing: Finding
a Home at the Water's Edge,* 2000

Servid, Carolyn and Snow, Don,
editors
The Book of the Tongass, 1999

**Williams, Terry Tempest and
Trimble, Stephen,** compilers
*Testimony: Writers of the West
Speak On Behalf of Utah
Wilderness,* 1996

Zwinger, Ann Haymond
*Shaped by Wind and Water:
Reflections of a Naturalist,* 2000

BOOKS FOR
YOUNG READERS

Armistead, John
The Return of Gabriel, 2002
ILLUSTRATIONS BY JOHN GREGORY
The $66 Summer, 2000

Buchwald, Emilie
Gildaen, 1993
ILLUSTRATIONS BY BARBARA FLYNN

Caldwell, V. M.
The Ocean Within, 1999
Tides, 2001

Douglas, Marjorie Stoneman
Alligator Crossing, 2003

Harrar, George
Parents Wanted, 2001
The Trouble with Jeremy Chance, 2003

Haugaard, Kay
No Place, 1998

Haynes, David
The Gumma Wars, 1997
West 7th Street Wildcats, 1997

Henderson, Aileen Kilgore
The Summer of the Bonepile Monster,
  1995
ILLUSTRATIONS BY KIM DAVID COOPER
The Monkey Thief, 1997
ILLUSTRATIONS BY PAUL MIROCHA
Treasure of Panther Peak, 1998
ILLUSTRATIONS BY KIM DAVID COOPER
Hard Times for Jake Smith, 2004

Lowell, Susan
I Am Lavina Cumming, 1993
ILLUSTRATIONS BY PAUL MIROCHA
The Boy with Paper Wings, 1995
ILLUSTRATIONS BY PAUL MIROCHA

Marvin, Isabel
A Bride for Anna's Papa, 1994

McGrory, Yvonne
The Secret of the Ruby Rings, 1994
ILLUSTRATIONS BY TERRY MYLER
Emma and the Ruby Ring, 2002
ILLUSTRATIONS BY TERRY MYLER

Schmidt, Annie M. G.
Minnie, 1994
ILLUSTRATIONS BY KAY SATHER
translated by Lance Salway

St. Antoine, Sara, editor
Stories from Where We Live
ILLUSTRATIONS BY TRUDY
  NICHOLSON
MAPS BY PAUL MIROCHA
The North Atlantic Coast, 2000
The California Coast, 2001
The Gulf Coast, 2002
The Great Lakes, 2003
The Great North American Prairie,
  2004

Wilbur, Frances
The Dog with Golden Eyes, 1998
ILLUSTRATIONS BY MARY COYLE

Williams, Laura E.
Behind the Bedroom Wall, 1996
ILLUSTRATIONS BY NANCY GOLDSTEIN
The Spider's Web, 1999
ILLUSTRATIONS BY BY ERICA MAGNUS

ACKNOWLEDGMENTS

In order to thrive, a nonprofit literary publisher relies on support and endorsement from a multitude. At this landmark time in Milkweed's history, I would like to recognize some of those who have made a difference to the press along the way.

First, to R. W. (Randy) Scholes, cofounder and partner: gratitude always for your expertise, artistry, and unflagging commitment during our collaborative journey.

Thanks to the writers I've had the pleasure of working with: for the time we've spent together, for the magic you create on the page, for your words and ideas that open minds and hearts—that shape and reshape views and opinions about why and for what purposes we lead our lives.

Thanks to librarians who, early on, found our titles worth including in their collections, to the independent bookstores who began—and continue—to stock our titles, to educators who teach Milkweed books to energize their high school and college students, and to reviewers who select the work of Milkweed authors that they believe is worthy of readers' attention.

Sincere appreciation to the individuals and to the private and public philanthropic organizations that have endorsed Milkweed's publishing mission with their support.

At a small press, publishing is a deeply collaborative process that depends on the commitment, motivation, and acumen of every staff member. Our staff has been consistently outstanding. It's been a real joy to take part with them in the process of making, marketing, and celebrating each new title. I would like to acknowledge our gratitude for the memory of Marilyn Matthews, a friend to all, for her consistent, beneficial work on behalf of Milkweed from the beginning until she retired in 2003.

Thanks, Linda Hoeschler, for being the energizing, spirited first Milkweed board member, and to Joanne Von Blon for being the second, a grand beginning. Our board members have advocated for Milkweed's mission with caring, insight, and the know-how that enabled us to move the press forward. Immense thanks to each, with major appreciation to those who took on the weighty commitment of being a board chair. From 1980–2003, the board chairs were (in alphabetical order): Susan Stauffer Blaser, Susan Borneman, Kathy Stevens Dougherty, Judith K. Healey, Randy Lebedoff, Dorothy K. Light, Margaret Robinson Preska, Debbie Reynolds, Cynthia Snyder, and Brenda Wehle.

Sincere appreciation to Debbie Meister for connecting Milkweed's books with local schools in her work as the coordinator of Milkweed's Alliance for Reading program.

Major thanks to critic and reviewer Brigitte Frase for years of peerless editorial consulting.

A shout-out of admiration for Scott Slovic, who introduced me to the world of environmental writing. Scott initiated and managed Milkweed's Credo series. He continues to teach and travel in the service of preserving and protecting the earth.

Because distribution is vital to a publisher, we thank Jim Sitter, founder of the magazine distributor Bookslinger, and later a founder of the Minnesota Center for Book Arts, for adding *Milkweed Chronicle* back in 1982 to the list of journals Bookslinger distributed. In 1985, when our first books were ready to send into the world, Consortium Book Sales and Distribution, founded by Bobbi Rix, became Milkweed Editions's distributor, vaulting the press to national outreach. At Consortium meetings we were introduced to the dedicated sales reps; there we met Stu Abraham, publishing professional and friend, whose discerning advice we always prize.

Compliments and huzzahs to our accommodating, meticulous production managers at Bookmobile over the years, Rachel Holscher, Sarah Purdy, Sarah Miner, and Connie Kuhnz.

Wholehearted thanks to Laurie Buss Herrmann, a former Milkweed Editions managing editor, for expertly proofreading this manuscript, as well as so many others.

I thank my husband, Henry Buchwald, partner in life and adventure, for being a primary source of encouragement, support, and wise counsel, gifts that have never diminished—and our children, for championing my work as a writer and publisher. They are bedrock.

Emilie Buchwald, PhD, was the founding copublisher and editor of *Milkweed Chronicle* and Milkweed Editions. She is the founding publisher, now copublisher, and editor of The Gryphon Press, children's picture books celebrating the human-animal bond. Books she has edited have received more than two hundred awards and recognitions.

Buchwald's book of poems, *The Moment's Only Moment*, is an IBPA Benjamin Franklin Award winner. She was editor of the Poetry Society of America's Wallace Stevens Centenary Celebration publication and the coeditor of three poetry anthologies.

She is the author of two children's novels, *Floramel and Esteban* (William Allen White Children's Book Master List) and *Gildaen* (Best Children's Book of the Year, Ages 9–12, Chicago Tribune Book Festival Award), and of two children's picture books under the name Daisy Bix: *At the Dog Park with Sam and Lucy* and *Buddy Unchained* (Henry Bergh Award, Best Children's Picture Book of the Year, and HSUS KIND Award, Best Children's Picture Book of the Year).

Buchwald is a recipient of the McKnight Distinguished Artist Award, the Kay Sexton Award, the A.P. Anderson Award, an honorary Doctor of Humane Letters degree from the University of Minnesota, and the National Book Critics Circle Ivan Sandrof Lifetime Achievement Award.

Emilie and her husband, Henry, live in Minneapolis.

milkweed
editions

Founded as a nonprofit organization in 1980, Milkweed
Editions is an independent publisher. Our mission is to
identify, nurture and publish transformative literature, and
build an engaged community around it.

Milkweed Editions is based in Bdé Óta Othúŋwe
(Minneapolis) within Mní Sota Makhóčhe, the traditional
homeland of the Dakhóta people. Residing here since
time immemorial, Dakhóta people still call Mní Sota
Makhóčhe home, with four federally recognized Dakhóta
nations and many more Dakhóta people residing in what
is now the state of Minnesota. Due to continued legacies
of colonization, genocide, and forced removal, generations
of Dakhóta people remain disenfranchised from their
traditional homeland. Presently, Mní Sota Makhóčhe has
become a refuge and home for many Indigenous nations
and peoples, including seven federally recognized Ojibwe
nations. We humbly encourage our readers to reflect upon
the historical legacies held in the lands they occupy.

milkweed.org